The Love Commandment

How to Find Its Meaning For Today

Mary W. Patrick

CBP Press
St. Louis, Missouri

© 1984 CBP Press

All rights reserved. No part of this book may be reproduced by any method without the publisher's written permission. Address: CBP Press, Box 179, St. Louis, MO 63166.

Unless otherwise indicated, all Scripture quotations are from the Revised Standard Version of the Bible, copyrighted 1946, 1952, © 1971, 1973.

Library of Congress Cataloging in Publication Data

Patrick, Mary W.
   The love commandment.

   Bibliography: p. 93
   1. Love (Theology)—Biblical teaching. 2. Ethics in the Bible. 3. Bible. N.T.—Criticism, interpretation, etc. I. Title.
BS2545.L6P37   1984   225.6   84-7083
ISBN 0-8272-2118-5

Manufactured in the United States of America

For
H.E.W. (1900-1968) and J.M.W.

Hear, O Israel: The LORD our God is one LORD; and you shall love the LORD your God with all your heart, and with all your soul, and with all your might (Deuteronomy 6:4-5).

You shall love your neighbor as yourself (Leviticus 19:18).

Foreword

This book is written for busy front-line pastors who don't have time to read much New Testament scholarship and for those laypeople who seek solid food. It begins with the perception that most such people—and they are the life-blood of the church—place the concept of love at the center of their theological and ethical thinking. I have attempted to offer to such people the wisdom of five different New Testament authors on this subject. I have proceeded exegetically, one passage at a time. I have tried to make my exegetical moves clear and to give reasons for my readings without burdening the reader with the baggage all scholars carry. An appendix at the end of the book discusses methodological issues in somewhat more detail.

I wrote the book but I had a lot of help. I lectured on these passages in 1980 during Lent at the First Presbyterian Church in Columbia, Missouri, our home for fourteen years, and then again in the fall of 1983 at Covenant Christian Church and Glen Echo Christian Church in Des Moines, Iowa, our current home. In the spring of 1982 Larry Bouchard and Dale Richesin, colleagues at Disciples Divinity House of the University of Chicago, insisted that I write an essay on the shape New Testament studies ought to take among Disciples of Christ in the future. I wrote on literary approaches to New Testament study and used the love commandment as my example. When Herb Lambert, the new editor of CBP Press, saw my essay, he encouraged me to write a short book on the love commandment using the literary approach I advocated.

Elder Gwen Lidstrom of Glen Echo Christian Church has read most of the manuscript, caught several substantial lapses of communication and made numerous stylistic suggestions. My husband, Dale Patrick, an Old Testament scholar, would have written this book differently and has had the good grace not to grind his favorite axes. He has busied himself instead with his own scholarship and teaching and with single-parenting our almost-teenage son, Jeremy. Readers who compare this book to his *Introduction to Biblical Law*, written some time before this book, will realize that conversation is very important in our house. Jim Kratz, pastor at Glen Echo Christian Church, and Donna Brown, the church secretary, have rearranged their schedules to accommodate the typing of the manuscript. Others not named here will find their story, metaphor or idea somewhere in the text without attribution. The contributions of all these people are gratefully acknowledged. The flaws and misreadings are my own.

Because we learn so much from those who teach us first, it seems appropriate to dedicate my first book to my parents, Ellis and Juanita Webber, both elders in the Presbyterian church and, admirably equipped with the clay feet God uses so well, models of service to their Lord.

Mary W. Patrick
Des Moines, Iowa
February 1984

Table of Contents

	Page
1 Interpretation "All the Way Down"	9
2 Jesus' Interpretation	19
3 Mark's Interpretation	32
4 Matthew's Interpretation	41
5 Luke's Interpretation	51
6 John's Interpretation	61
7 Paul's Interpretation	70
8 How to Find the Meaning for Today	84
Appendix Literary Approaches to the Study of the Bible	89
Notes	93

1

Interpretation "All the Way Down"

Once upon a time in a land far away, a child asked a parent a deep and important question, "What holds the world up?" The parent replied firmly, "Someone with big hands holds the world up."

The child seemed satisfied with the answer but returned after a time to ask, "But what holds up the big-hands person?" The parent answered, "The big-hands person stands on a horse."

Not much time had passed when the child returned to inquire, "And what holds up the horse?" "Oh," replied the parent, "the horse stands on the back of a very large elephant."

Puzzled, the child asked again, "And what holds up the elephant?" Patiently the parent explained, "The second elephant holds up the first elephant."

Tentatively, carefully, the child tested an interpretation, "And does a third elephant hold up the second elephant?" "Yes, my child," replied the parent, "from there on it's all elephants, elephants all the way down."

The story about "elephants all the way down" isn't a new story. I didn't make it up. On the other hand, it may not be a very old story either. It is, rather, a perennial story. Like a perennial in the garden, it blooms each year with a perennial problem and a perennial nonanswer which may be the best answer yet. The question is very common and comes in several varieties:

What are the underlying factors?
Can we reconstruct the chain of events?
What stands behind . . . ?
How did we get where we are today?
Why don't we get to the bottom of this?

The answer is also common enough to be called perennial: The farther you look the more you can see, and there is no end in sight.

Interpretation works like the elephants in the story. Scarcely a sentence can be written that doesn't interpret something. And the interpretation can itself be interpreted. And soon we have an interpretation of an interpretation of an interpretation with no end in sight, interpretation all the way down.

The Case of the Multiple Text

The New Testament is full of interpretations of the Old Testament. This is not surprising. The Old Testament was the first Bible of the Christian church. It was read, mostly in a Greek translation, enjoyed, meditated on, and, above all, remembered. Some scholarly people selected Old Testament materials by which to interpret the teachings, the activities, or the death and resurrection of Jesus, or some aspect of life as a Christian, and wrote Gospels and letters for Christians to read. What the authors did would have made no sense if the early Christian readers had not been well acquainted with the Old Testament narratives and poetry. I can't imagine people bothering to read the Gospel of Matthew, to mention the most prominent example, unless they were already big fans of the Old Testament.

The Gospel of Matthew is not the only place in the New Testament where we find interpretations of the Old Testament, but it has plenty of examples for our purposes here. Matthew makes a beautiful tapestry at the beginning of his Gospel, weaving together quotations from the Old Testament to create a picture of Jesus' birth and early years. He introduces the first of these with the formula, "All this took place to fulfill what the Lord had spoken by the prophet" (1:22), and repeats the formula, with some variations, no less than seven times before he begins the story of Jesus' ministry with the words "From that time Jesus began to preach," in 4:17.

You don't have to confine yourself to the place where Matthew uses his formula to find him interpreting the Old Testament. Notice that Matthew tells us in the very first verse that he intends to link Jesus to two major heroes of the Old Testament, David and Abraham: "The book of the genealogy of Jesus Christ, the son of David, the son of Abraham" (Matthew 1:1). That first verse is a kind of title to the book, and Matthew's thesis for the whole book is that Jesus is the legitimate heir of David and Abraham. What was promised in their stories is fulfilled in Jesus' story. That's the way Matthew sees Jesus; that's the way he tells Jesus' story.

The most famous example of the fact that the New Testament interprets the Old Testament is found in Matthew 5—7, the Sermon on the Mount. The theme of at least part of the sermon is found in 5:17, "Think not that I have come to abolish the law and the prophets; I have come not to abolish them but to fulfil them." This sermon will describe fulfilling the law and the prophets.

The phrase "the law and the prophets" was the title of the Bible at the time of Jesus. The phrase refers to two sections of the Jewish Bible. "The Law" is the first five books of the Old Testament; "the prophets" refers to the history books (Joshua, Judges, 1 and 2 Samuel, 1 and 2 Kings) and all the books which bear the names of prophets. The rest of the books in the Old Testament were read extensively but were not counted as part of the Bible until shortly after the time the New Testament books were written.

The remainder of chapter 5 should tell us what it means to "fulfil" the law and the prophets. We find six antitheses which begin, "You have heard that it was said to the men of old . . . But I say to you . . ." (Matthew 5:21-22). The formula varies only slightly at each repetition. Following the first part of the formula is a quotation either from the Old Testament or from interpretation well known to the first audience. For example, the first quotation quotes the fifth commandment, "You shall not kill," and also quotes the explanation that went with it, "and whoever kills shall be liable to judgment" (Matthew 5:21 quotes Exodus 20:13 and an interpretation). The second quotation, by contrast, is directly from the Ten Commandments, "You shall not commit adultery" (Matthew 5:27 quotes Exodus 20:14), without any explanation.

The second part of each antithesis is Jesus' own interpretation using the formula "But I say to you . . . ." Each time he prohibits the secret disposition of the heart which manifests itself in the outward behavior, "But I say to you that every one who is angry with his brother shall be liable to judgment" (Matthew 5:22). Sometimes, as in the two examples we have looked at, he also prohibits those minor activities which are a miniature of the major ones—murder and adultery—"Whoever insults his brother shall be liable" (Matthew 5:22) and "Every one who looks at a woman lustfully has already committed adultery with her in his heart" (Matthew 5:28).

Jesus thinks of the history of the interpretation of these Old Testament passages as a process of relaxing the commandments, of making excuses. By his reckoning, limiting commandments to prohibitions of things you never do anyway and making excuses is the way to abolish the law and the prophets. "Whoever then relaxes one of the least of these commandments and teaches men so, shall be called least in the kingdom of heaven" (Matthew 5:19). His own interpretation reverses that trend. No more excuses.

It is clear that in the Sermon on the Mount we see an interpretation of Old Testament texts by Jesus. We even find the word "fulfil" that we also saw in Matthew 1 and 2. In relation to Jesus' early life, Matthew constructs a history of salvation by a process of interpretation, linking past to present. In relation to Jesus' teaching in the Sermon on the Mount, however, I don't think a "history of salvation" describes what is going on. Jesus' interpretation doesn't so much link past to present as jump over the past.

What does "fulfil" mean in the Sermon on the Mount? I propose that it means "go back to what God intended all along." God did not intend to permit lust and anger and then to prohibit their outward expression. Nor did God intend to permit insults and minor "skirt chasing" and then to prohibit their large-scale social manifestations. Rather, says Jesus, God intended even the most excitable people to cultivate that peace of mind which is not disposed to aggression of any kind. Going back to what God intended is not a matter of abolishing the law but of fulfilling it.

When the authors of the New Testament thought of interpreting Old Testament passages, they took their place in a long line of interpreters. We can see authors of Old Testament books interpreting Old Testament stories of earlier times. The example that comes most readily to mind is the story of the

Exodus. Because the story of the Exodus is long and complicated, I will select only one small incident from it, the crossing of the Red Sea, to illustrate the point that the Old Testament already interprets Old Testament stories.

As Moses led the people of Israel out of Egypt they came to the sea with the Egyptian army in hot pursuit. At the Lord's command Moses divided the sea. The people of Israel walked through on dry land with the Egyptians close behind. Again at the Lord's command, Moses closed up the sea and the Egyptians drowned. This story is in Exodus 14.

The story of the crossing of the Jordan River to get into the promised land is told as an interpretation of the deliverance at the sea. This story is in Joshua 3 and 4. On the instructions of the Lord, Joshua commands the priests to step into the river carrying the ark of the covenant. When they do, the river stops flowing and the people cross on dry land. After the people are on the other side, the priests with the ark step out and the river flows as usual. Joshua has a stone monument to the crossing set up and dedicates it. In describing the dedication speech, the author makes clear the connection of the two crossings:

> And he said to the people of Israel, "When your children ask their fathers in time to come, 'What do these stones mean?' then you shall let your children know, 'Israel passed over this Jordan on dry ground.' For the LORD your God dried up the waters of the Jordan for you until you passed over, as the LORD your God did to the Red Sea, which he dried up for us until we passed over, so that all the peoples of the earth may know that the hand of the LORD is mighty" (Joshua 4:21-24).

To this point we have looked at a story interpreting a story. Stories can also be interpreted in poems. There is one psalm that interprets the crossing of the Red Sea and the crossing of the Jordan as a single act of salvation.

> The sea looked and fled,
>   Jordan turned back.
> What ails you, O sea, that you flee?
>   O Jordan, that you turn back?
> Tremble, O earth, at the presence of the LORD,
>   At the presence of the God of Jacob. (Psalm 114:3,5,7)

The Old Testament prophets interpreted the story of the escape from Egypt extensively. They point to the Exodus as evidence of God's ability to do new acts of salvation. The past is cited as a guarantee of the present and the future. This was an especially important message before, during, and after the time when Israel was in exile in Babylon. The prophet who wrote from Babylon near the end of the Exile saw the exodus from Egypt as a model for the new exodus from Babylon, an event he expected any day. In this passage he refers to the crossing of the sea.

> Thus says the LORD,
>   who makes a way in the sea,
>   a path in the mighty waters,
> who brings forth chariot and horse,
>   army and warrior;

> they lie down, they cannot rise,
>   they are extinguished, quenched like a wick:
> "Remember not the former things,
>   nor consider the things of old.
> Behold, I am doing a new thing;
>   now it springs forth, do you not perceive it?
> I will make a way in the wilderness
>   and rivers in the desert." (Isaiah 43:16-19)

When New Testament authors interpret the Old Testament they often use a technique of direct quotation. That is, you will find a verse from the Old Testament in quotation marks and then some comments on it. In the example we looked at, when authors of Old Testament texts interpret an Old Testament story, they do not use direct quotation. Rather, they retell the story or refer to it in a phrase. They want to call attention, not to a verse or a passage, but to a story or to the central action of the story.

Do New Testament authors interpret the New Testament? If they do, do they interpret it by direct quotation or do they interpret it by retelling, or referring to, a story? Or do they interpret both ways and some others besides? The answer is: Yes, all of the above.

New Testament authors are so set on talking about Jesus and the significance of Jesus that it would be surprising if they didn't interpret one another. Matthew, Mark, and Luke contain long stretches of words and sentences that are identical. The usual explanation, which appears to me to be generally correct, is that Matthew and Luke copied from Mark, added some stories Mark didn't include, and tied the whole together into a distinctive package. You could say that Matthew is partly the author's interpretation of the life of Jesus and partly the author's interpretation of Mark's interpretation of the life of Jesus. Luke begins his Gospel by telling us that he is evaluating books and pamphlets already in circulation:

> Inasmuch as many have undertaken to compile a narrative of the things which have been accomplished among us, just as they were delivered to us by those who from the beginning were eyewitnesses and ministers of the word, it seemed good to me also, having followed all things closely for some time past, to write an orderly account for you, most excellent Theophilus, that you may know the truth concerning the things of which you have been informed (Luke 1:1-4).

Careful reading of his Gospel would tell us that this author thinks what we call the Gospel of Mark is the best of the lot.

Paul wrote his letters before there were Gospels to quote verses from. How, we may ask ourselves, could it be possible for the first author in the New Testament to be an interpreter? The answer is that Paul reflects on the significance of Jesus, especially of Jesus' death and resurrection. He does this primarily by inserting statements beginning with "who" after a reference to Jesus, as you can see in the first verses of his letter to the Galatians:

> Paul an apostle—not from men nor through man, but through Jesus Christ and God the Father, who raised him from the dead—and all the brethren who are with me, To the churches of Galatia:

> Grace to you and peace from God the Father and our Lord Jesus Christ, who gave himself for our sins (Galatians 1:1-4).

In this passage Paul has interpreted the resurrection of first Jesus and then the crucifixion, each with its own "who" statement. Paul interprets the death and resurrection directly, in this passage, without saying he knows of anyone else who has ever said anything similar about Jesus. My guess is, however, that phrases at the beginning of a letter will be references to something the addressees already know very well.

In another famous passage, Paul quotes word for word the interpretation of earlier Christians:

> For I delivered to you as of first importance what I also received, that Christ died for our sins in accordance with the scriptures, that he was buried, that he was raised on the third day in accordance with the scriptures, and that he appeared to ... (1 Corinthians 15:3-5).

The formula "What I also received" is the clue that Paul is quoting an interpretation done previously by someone else. The phrase "in accordance with the scriptures," which is repeated twice, shows that the interpretation Paul quotes is already an interpretation of the Old Testament. Paul quotes the passage and then goes on to interpret it, spelling out its implications through the remainder of a long and very beautiful chapter.

More examples could be given. But the ones we have looked at have shown that, yes indeed, the New Testament authors are interpreters. All of them reflect on the significance of Jesus and in that sense are interpreters of Jesus' life, death, and resurrection. In addition, we have seen that Matthew and Luke interpret Mark, and Paul interprets a Christian teaching about the resurrection of Jesus that he received from earlier Christians. The teaching Paul received with its sequence died—buried—was raised—appeared is the plot line of a story which wasn't written out, as far as we know, in Paul's day but which we can read in the stories at the end of the Gospels, written a generation later.

The case of the multiple text is a case in which no author stands at the beginning of the story he tells. New Testament authors interpret the Old Testament; Old Testament authors retell the Old Testament; New Testament authors interpret the New Testament. Even Paul, the earliest New Testament author, was an interpreter of still earlier unwritten teachings. The multiple text is an interpretation of an interpretation of an interpretation. Like the elephants in the story, each one upon the back of yet another with no end in sight, the case of the multiple text is elephants all the way down.

The most important instance of a multiple text is the command given by Jesus to love God and neighbor. It is one of the most famous passages in the whole Bible. Generations of Sunday school children learned it by heart and many adult Christians still remember it. Try an experiment: See if you can still recite it. If you got it right, I will guess that you recited Matthew 22:37-39 or some part of it. If you got it sort of right, I will guess that you mixed Matthew with Mark or Luke.

Let's put these three versions in parallel columns.

Matthew 22:37-39	**Mark 12:30-31**	**Luke 10:27**
You shall love the Lord your God with all your heart, and with all your soul, and with all your mind.	You shall love the Lord your God with all your heart, and with all your soul, and with all your mind, and with all your strength.	You shall love the Lord your God with all your heart, and with all your soul, and with all your strength, and with all your mind;
This is the great and first commandment. And a second is like it, You shall love your neighbor as yourself.	The second is this, You shall love your neighbor as yourself.	and your neighbor as yourself.

All three Gospels agree on the basics: Jesus said two things: 1) "You shall love the Lord your God," and 2) "You shall love your neighbor as yourself" except that Luke leaves out "You shall love" the second time. The Gospels differ on the number of inner parts with which you are to love God and the order in which they are to be enumerated. They also differ in the story used as the setting for the love commandment and the phrases or sentences put in the middle.

We have three distinct interpretations of something Jesus said. We will inspect each interpretation later in this book. Chapter 3 will be devoted to Mark 12:28-34, chapter 4 to Matthew 22:34-40 and some other passages, and chapter 5 to Luke 10:25-37. The three interpretations are interrelated, and the similarities are at least as interesting as the differences.

What Jesus said, according to all three Gospels, was a quotation of two widely separated verses in the Old Testament, Deuteronomy 6:5 and Leviticus 19:18. We will inspect Jesus' interpretation in chapter 2. At present it is enough to note that the love commandment is an example of how the New Testament interprets the Old Testament as well as an example of how New Testament authors interpret Jesus.

Two other parts of the New Testament also interpret the love commandment. As we will see in chapter 6, the Gospel of John treats it quite differently from the other Gospels. Paul quotes only the second half of Jesus' love commandment, the part about the neighbor, in Romans 13:9. However, as we will see in chapter 7, I think that Paul's interpretation of the love commandment is not limited to his explicit quotations. Both John and Paul reflect profoundly on the meaning of the love commandment. Their theological reflections are both more profound and more extensive than you would guess from counting the number of times they quote Deuteronomy 6:5 and Leviticus 19:18.

I believe the love commandment was as familiar to first-century Christians as it is to modern Christians. The authors of the New Testament and the first readers thought long and hard about its implications for their lives, just as Christians have from that day to this. The chapters which follow will interpret Jesus' interpretation, and New Testament interpretations of Jesus' interpretation, for modern readers.

The Case of the Multiple Reader

People perceive things differently. What is politeness on one side of the world is downright rudeness on the other. One generation likes mellifluous strings; another, the electric twang of an amplified guitar. Some Christians look for a church with "smells and bells," while other Christians seek out plain speaking. Large-scale cultural differences among national groups exist, and so do generation gaps and many other kinds of diversity. We have different points of view, different perspectives. All of these divisions make it difficult for us to communicate, much less to agree, even when we all speak English.

Not only is there diversity within the human community; there is also diversity, and a certain amount of tension, in each individual human. Who am I? Am I a writer, woman, scholar, consumer, mother, wife, thinker, educator, Christian, student, city-dweller, volunteer or budget-balancer? All of the above. But in a different order every day. I live by juggling roles. Often I drop one, and the effort to pick it up again makes a mess of the whole juggling act. Your life is probably like that, too. Maybe you juggle different roles, and perhaps you juggle them so automatically that you never have to think about it. But the roles we play, and the priority we give to any particular role, may differentiate us decisively. Of course, roles aren't our only components. We also have values and commitments, attitudes and experiences, competences and expectations. We're all so complicated it's a wonder we can communicate at all.

The case of the multiple reader is the case of readers who belong to several groupings in society and who bring to a book like this one, or to a passage like the love commandment, a complicated mix of roles and values. The point is often made that what you get out of a passage depends on who you are and what you bring to the reading. I would add the reminder, and this point is not made as often, that who the reader is and what the reader brings is an exceedingly complicated matter, about as complicated as a story which is an interpretation of an interpretation of an interpretation.

How Interpretation Works

Interpretation is an act of imagination which we all perform regularly. Let me give you a simple example. If I tell you that as a child I went to a place called Blue Rock Springs where there is a big drinking fountain at the entrance to the park and that I discovered there that, although the water looks all right, it smells awful and tastes worse, you will begin right away to interpret the story. Recalling similar childhood experiences, you may wrinkle up your nose sympathetically and say "Yuck." Or you may supply some background about mineral springs. Or a few of you may even supply additional memories of the same place, saying something about eucalyptus trees, tadpoles, or church picnics.

We should be able to identify some characteristic acts of imagination to use in the task of interpretation. Let me suggest a few.

Reliving. This is the most common strategy for interpreting stories about childhood, romance, or the common experiences of life.

Entering into Possible Worlds. This is the most common strategy for interpreting stories which take place in distant places or times, whether real or not.

Application. This is the most common strategy for interpreting stories of danger, heroism, or other extreme situations. What would I have done? How would I have survived or conquered or helped?

Juxtaposition. This common strategy involves setting something you already know, perhaps from the Bible, alongside a new story, illuminating both. The trick is to think of the right combination of things to juxtapose.

Accumulation. This common strategy involves letting something you already know, perhaps from the Bible or your own life, influence your perception of a new story.

New Readings. This common strategy involves returning to a well-known story with eyes open in some new way, that sees differently or sees more than on previous readings.

We could add more items to this list of the characteristics of the act of interpretation if we tried. None of these is unfamiliar. You might not need any but the first to interpret adequately the story I told about an encounter with a drinking fountain at Blue Rock Springs. But if I elaborated on the story, some other interpretive strategies might become necessary.

If we take not a simple example from my childhood, but a story from the Bible, we will need all the interpretive strategies we can get. The act of interpretation is the same for the Bible as for the simplest story. The exercise of imagination is the same. What is different is the complexity and profundity of the story and the enormous importance we attach to it. If God is the main character and the plot line has to do with the preservation and eventual salvation of all humanity, it is of the utmost importance that we get it right. Even if our own salvation doesn't depend on our understanding, the adequacy of our witness in word and deed certainly does.

No one will object if I use the term "imagination" when I offer a story from my childhood for your interpretation, but I'm quite sure someone will object to the term in relation to the Bible. "Imagination," someone will say, "is for kids. Imagination means something is fantasy, not reality. It's for frivolous stories and immature minds. We ought to think seriously, with principles and facts and ideals, not fiddle around with games and fantasy."

The answer to such an objection is twofold: (1) The concepts in the Bible are always embedded in stories. If you ignore the story, you will misunderstand the concepts; (2) Imagination is the only way to get inside a story. If you don't get inside the story, you won't know what it means. A disciplined imagination is attentive to the distinct nuance or subtle quality of the story it works on, and it makes use of the logic of what is being interpreted. A disciplined imagination is indispensable for interpreting the Bible.

Interpretation has occurred when three things have happened: (1) A reader with an active mind and a full life has come to a story; (2) An imaginary tour of the world of the story has been undertaken; and (3) The reader has appropriated the story, making it part of an enriched life. Let me comment on each of the three in turn. There is, first of all, a reader with all the complexity of someone putting all sorts of values and commitments into practice while juggling a variety of roles. This reader has some reason to read a story, say one in the Bible, a question worth asking or reasking. A reader is never a blank page onto which an author puts words or ideas. A reader is not a silent listener to an author's monologue. Rather, the reader is an active participant with the author in a dialogue about the meaning of a story.

The second phase of interpretation is an imaginary excursion into the world of the story. In the case of the Bible, this excursion is quite a complicated matter and is likely to scare off many a reader. Scholars spend years of their lives learning languages, geography, history of relevant cultures, and history of literature in order to make just such excursions. When the story in question is, like the story of the love commandment, not a single story but an interpretation of an interpretation of an interpretation with no end in sight, the perplexities multiply. It is the function of books like this one to offer guided tours of what one famous theologian called "the strange new world of the Bible," exploring its highways and byways, noting the scenery and the architecture, the ornamentation and the interpretation, and to do it all without getting lost.

By the time you have finished this book, phase three, the appropriation of the story, the incorporation of it into your life and thought will be under way. The task of appropriation will take you far beyond the covers of this book. Chapter 8 will offer some suggestions about the process of appropriation.

For the next six chapters we will travel together on a guided tour of the world of the love commandment. We begin by considering Jesus' commandment separately from what any New Testament author wrote about it. Then we will take up what five different authors of New Testament books wrote about what Jesus commanded and what Jesus meant by what he said. The tour is ready to begin. All aboard!

2

Jesus' Interpretation

In this chapter we begin our excursion into the love commandment. We will need to be very clear about where the road is going and which turn to take at each crossroads. When we return from our excursion we want to know where we have been. We certainly don't want to get lost.

The results of this chapter can be stated at the beginning: *Jesus put Deuteronomy 6:4-5 and Leviticus 19:18 together and gave them great importance.* This result is not very startling but it contains a whole bag of puzzling questions. Let me ask some of them.

1) How do we know it was Jesus who stated the love commandment?
2) What can we say about the two verses from the Old Testament in themselves?
3) What kind of interpretive act is it to put two verses together? How do they influence each other?
4) What does his giving great importance to these two verses say about Jesus' relation to debates about the Old Testament law?

We will take up these questions in turn in the course of this chapter.

You will note that this first part of our excursion leads us to Jesus' own ministry and to the people who heard his words directly. The next chapters will lead us to the early churches, where Jesus' love commandment was clarified and interpreted by New Testament authors for the life of church members. Here we are looking through their interpretation to see if we can see the Jesus they saw.

A century ago, scholars worked very hard to jump over the interpretations of Jesus which we find in the New Testament, to get to Jesus himself. They wrote biographies of Jesus and studies which spoke of the plain and simple teachings of Jesus and the distortions of later authors. The great Albert Schweitzer wrote a book called *The Quest for the Historical Jesus,* in which he showed the failure of these attempts to get to Jesus himself. The "historical" Jesus nineteenth-century scholars found looks entirely too much like a nineteenth-century scholar! Trying to jump over the New Testament interpretations they saw not Jesus, but reflections of themselves.

On our excursion through the world of the love commandment, as we try to see Jesus and hear what he said to his original audience, we need to be aware that we are walking on thin ice. Can we avoid seeing nothing more than reflections of ourselves when we try to see Jesus? A great deal of thought has gone into techniques for avoiding the errors of the past. We have come to realize that the only way to get to Jesus is through the New Testament stories. Let me put it another way: Interpretation of the New Testament is the only way to get to the historical Jesus.

Question #1: *How do we know it was Jesus who stated something, such as the love commandment, that is attributed to him in the New Testament?* This may seem like a silly question. The stories, after all, set out what they want us to observe. Clearly, the stories want us to observe Jesus' saying what they say he said. The question arises because in this chapter we aren't looking *at* the stories in the New Testament. Rather, we are looking *through* them to see what is behind them. Is there really a historical Jesus back there quoting Deuteronomy 6:4-5 and Leviticus 19:18? Remember that the stories about Jesus were told and retold for a whole generation before any of our Gospels was written. The process of telling and retelling stories can alter them pretty drastically, and it was in this process that things got attributed to Jesus that he didn't say. We have to reckon with the possibilities that Jesus was misquoted, that things other people said got mixed in with things Jesus said, that things people said to explain what Jesus meant got attached to what Jesus said, and that a whole range of other possible alterations occurred in the process of retelling. We even have to reckon with pious fraud, people putting into Jesus' mouth what Jesus should have said, or would have said if he had faced another situation. It is because this first part of our tour of the love commandment takes us behind the stories to the real Jesus, who did and said real things, that we have to ask how to identify the authentic sayings.

The best way I know to show that Jesus really did put together Deuteronomy 6:4-5 and Leviticus 19:18 and give them great importance involves three criteria. Let's look at each criterion in turn.

1. The first criterion is this: Anything which appears in all or most of the sources of the Gospels and also elsewhere in the New Testament may be regarded as authentic. Does the love commandment meet this criterion? Of course it does. It appears in all four Gospels, several places in the letters of Paul, and some other places in the New Testament. That was easy, wasn't it?

2. The second criterion is harder: The earliest form of a saying may be regarded as authentic if it can be shown that neither first-century Jews nor first-century Christians would have invented it. Because Mark is the oldest Gospel, it is likely, on general principles, that his version of the love commandment will be the earliest. In chapter 3 we will see that Mark's is the earliest form of the love commandment. We will also find that no first-century Christian could possibly have invented Mark's story and that a first-cen-

tury Jew is not very likely to have invented it. Does the love commandment meet this second criterion for an authentic saying of the historical Jesus? Yes, it does, but you will have to read chapter 3 to get the details.

3. The third criterion is: Any other saying from the earliest tradition which uses different words to say the same thing as a saying which meets the second criterion may also be regarded as authentic. We won't need this criterion for the love commandment, for it already meets the second criterion.

I think we have now answered our first question. How do we know it was Jesus who issued the commandment to love God and neighbor? The answer is that almost every segment of the New Testament knows of it, and neither first-century Jews nor first-century Christians would be likely to have invented the earliest version. That is, the love commandment meets the first criterion and the second criterion for authentic sayings of Jesus. This is not a borderline case. The double command to love God and neighbor is properly classified as an authentic saying of the historical Jesus.

Question #2: If we have agreed that the love commandment belongs to the historical Jesus, we are ready to go on to the content of the commandment. *What can we say about the two verses from the Old Testament in themselves?*

Deuteronomy 6:4-5 summarizes the faith of Israel in a short, easily-remembered statement suitable for public recitation: "Hear, O Israel: The LORD our God is one LORD; and you shall love the LORD your God with all your heart, and with all your soul, and with all your might." To this day the words are as familiar to Jews as the pledge of allegiance to the flag is to American citizens or the Lord's Prayer and the Doxology are to Christian churchgoers. Like the Doxology and the Lord's Prayer, these verses have a title. They are called the *Shema* (with the accent on the last syllable), from the Hebrew word for "hear." They have formed Jewish identity through centuries of repetition in worship and education; they express Jewish identity in the present and connect modern Jews to their remote past.

If we look at the sentences which follow the Shema, we can see that they were intended to form the consciousness of the people who read them:

> And these words which I command you this day shall be upon your heart; and you shall teach them diligently to your children, and shall talk of them when you sit in your house, and when you walk by the way, and when you lie down, and when your rise. And you shall bind them as a sign upon your hand, and they shall be as frontlets between your eyes. And you shall write them on the doorposts of your house and on your gates" (Deuteronomy 6:6-9).

Notice that the words are to be "on your heart." These words are to be an inner law which is so much a part of you that it regulates your behavior from the inside. At the same time it is a public tradition which can and must be taught to the next generation. It can and must be thought about and talked about with other adults. It is to be the subject of meditation at evening and morning prayers. By the way, the Jewish custom of beginning a day at sunset is reflected here in the order "when you lie down and when you rise."

The final sentences have given rise to two Jewish customs, the use of phylacteries and the Mezuah. Phylacteries are small black boxes, containing tiny scrolls with words of the Shema and having long straps with which to bind them on the forehead and hand while praying at home. The Mezuzah is a tiny scroll containing the words of the Shema, which hangs beside the front door of many Jewish homes. These little scrolls remind Jews of their heritage and identity in the same way that crosses remind Christians of theirs. Some Christians wear crosses on chains around their necks or put them on the wall of their house or, as in my house, on the mantel. Deuteronomy 6:6-9 is about what laypeople do in their own homes and families to cultivate their own spiritual intensity and to educate their children. It does not depend on clergy, services, places of worship, or any official authorization.

We can see in Deuteronomy 6:6-9 that the Shema was intended to be what it in fact became, a symbol and summary of the faith of Israel. It has both an outward aspect, as a symbol for the doorpost and something to discuss and teach, and an inward aspect, as inner regulation of the wellsprings of thought and action. When we find Jesus quoting it, we know he is quoting something at the very center of the religious tradition of his first audience.

If we look at the Shema closely, we can see something of the content of that tradition. It begins with a personal address: "Hear, O Israel." Whoever recites the Shema is the teacher of Israel of every generation; whoever hears it is addressed personally and solemnly, as part of a large community, extending through space and time. When the Shema is recited in unison everyone fills both roles. The personal address seeks the involvement of the hearer in a concentrated and intense way. We will find the same concentration and intensity, the same total involvement, everywhere we look in our excursion through the love commandment. This is the first time, but not the last.

After the address comes a confession of faith, "The LORD our God is one LORD." This is the RSV translation, which goes on to list three alternative translations in the footnotes:

    The LORD our God, the LORD is one.
    The LORD is our God, the LORD is one.
    The LORD is our God, the LORD alone.

The various translations proposed give different emphases, but they are all possible translations of the Hebrew words. The sentence in Hebrew consists of four words in this order:

1. "The Lord," the traditional Jewish euphemism for the personal name, Yahweh
2. "our God"
3. "The Lord"
4. "one," a little word which can also mean "alone" or "only."

You will notice right away that there is no Hebrew word here to translate "is." In Hebrew it is possible to have a sentence without "is," but to translate such a sentence into English you have to supply "is." The question for translators of this sentence is: Where do you put it? There are four possibilities. You can put "is" between words 1 and 2, between words 2 and 3, between words 3 and 4, or in two places, between words 1 and 2 and between words 3 and 4. Your choice depends on what emphasis you want in English. The RSV committee followed the lead of the older King James translation because Bible readers know it so well. But we need to look at all the possible emphases because all are present in the Hebrew (and also in the Greek translations) and therefore were present to Jesus and to his first audience.

What happens if we put "is" between words 1 and 2, so that it reads "The Lord is our God, the Lord alone"? Now we have a statement of *exclusive belonging to this God* and to no other, with the emphasis on "*our* God."

The emphasis shifts if we put "is" between words 2 and 3 so that it reads, as the RSV does, "The Lord our God is one Lord." Now we have a statement of the *unity of God* with the emphasis on "one." If we put "is" between words 3 and 4 so that it reads "The Lord our God, the Lord is one," we get another statement of the unity of God with the emphasis on "one."

It is possible to get a neat balance between a statement of exclusive belonging to God and a statement of the unity of God by putting "is" in two places, between words 1 and 2 and between words 3 and 4. The resulting sentence reads "The Lord is our God, the Lord is one."

There is one other possible set of translations. What if we translate the third word "alone" or "only" instead of "one," so that it reads "The Lord our God is the only Lord" or " The Lord our God, the Lord is alone"? Now we have a statement of the *sole deity of God.* Nothing and no one except the Lord has a right to be called God.

We have found three kinds of statements that the four Hebrew words in the confession make: a statement of exclusive belonging, a statement of the unity of God and a statement of the sole deity of God. Israel confesses all three when the Shema is recited; all three are implied when Jesus quotes the Shema.

Two other aspects of the confession require our attention here. The first is that the third word, translated "one" or "alone" or "only," is another of the concentrating and intensifying terms we will meet again and again on this excursion through the love commandment.

Finally, we should observe that the confession "The Lord our God is one Lord" is an interpretation of the first of the Ten Commandments, "You shall have no other gods before me" (Exodus 20:3; Deuteronomy 5:7). For our purposes, this means that when Jesus interprets the Shema, he is already interpreting an interpretation.

After a personal address and a confession of faith in Deuteronomy 6:4 the Shema continues in 6:5 with the commandment "and you shall love the Lord your God." The word "love" is used a great many times in Deuteronomy and a longer passage can help us understand the character of love:

> It is because the LORD loves you, and is keeping the oath which he swore to your fathers, that the LORD has brought you out with a mighty hand, and redeemed you from the house of bondage, from the hand of Pharaoh king of Egypt. Know therefore that the LORD your God is God, the faithful God who keeps covenant and steadfast love with those who love him and keep his commandments, to a thousand generations (Deuteronomy 7:8-9).

In this passage we can see that love is God's motivation for rescuing Israel from Egypt. That means that love is characteristic of God's own nature. People who love God respond to God's love. They participate in God's nature and activity. So the command to love God is a command to respond to God by living in a way corresponding to the nature of God.

It is very odd to be commanded to love. In English the term "love" carries with it connotations of spontaneity that can't be commanded or coerced. The Greek translators of Deuteronomy had the same problem with the term. But they were fortunate enough to have three words for love. One Greek word for love is the word from which our English word "erotic" comes. You know, love as in love and marriage, the ones that "go together like a horse and carriage." Such love can neither be commanded nor coerced. There probably are erotic overtones to the love of God, but the Greek translators of Deuteronomy didn't want to overemphasize them, so they didn't use that word for love.

The second Greek term for love is the friendship term. The first part of the name Philadelphia, the city of brotherly love, comes from this word. There was a great deal of thinking and writing in Greek about the nature and requirements of true friendship. True friendship can't be commanded or coerced, but there are requirements which must be met before spontaneous friendship can take place. One of the requirements for the best kind of friendship is equality. Are we equal in any way to God? By no means. Friendship between unequals can't be of the highest kind; it can only be a friendship based on utility and benefits to be derived. Clearly, Deuteronomy isn't about this inferior kind of friendship. So the Greek translators of Deuteronomy didn't use the friendship word for love.

The third Greek word for love was little used and had few built-in associations. That word was *agape* (pronounced ah-GAH-pay), a word with which some Christians have become so familiar that they use it as if it were an English word. It seemed to meet the need of the Greek translators of Deuteronomy, and they used it often. *Agape* means what Deuteronomy says. It takes its meaning from the use right here in the Old Testament. It refers to the love which is part of God's own nature, to which we respond and on which we pattern our lives. New Testament writers picked up the word from the Greek Old Testament.

In the Shema the command to love God stands alone, as if there were no concrete, socially-observable obligations at all. When you think about how many laws there are in the Old Testament it is odd to find this command standing alone. The phrase "those who love him and keep his commandments" (Deuteronomy 7:9) suggests, however, that all the other laws express love of God in concrete terms, or, to put it another way, that keeping the commandments expresses your love of God. In that case, the commandment to love God in the Shema is an abbreviation.

There is one more section to the Shema. Not only is there a command to love God; there is also a command to love God "with all your heart, and with all your soul, and with all your might"—three parts. In the Gospels we find some confusion on what Jesus said when he quoted this part of Deuteronomy 6:5. Here, in the form of a table, are the words.

Deuteronomy 6:5	Matthew 22:37	Mark 12:30	Luke 10:27
heart	heart	heart	heart
soul	soul	soul	soul
	mind	mind	strength
might		strength	mind

All the Gospels agree with Deuteronomy 6:5 on the first two items, "with all your heart and with all your soul." The differences occur at the end of the list. We may agree that "might" is rather like "strength," something the body has or doesn't have. The problem is "mind." Where did "mind" come from?

The Hebrew language has no word for "mind." Thinking was said to be done with the heart, as in "But to this day the LORD has not given you a mind [Hebrew: heart] to understand, or eyes to see, or ears to hear" (Deuteronomy 29:4). By contrast, Greeks thought of people as being composed of three parts: body, mind and spirit or soul. The body acts, the mind thinks, the spirit or soul decides. By the time of Jesus, most people thought like the Greeks: body, mind, spirit. When they looked at Deuteronomy 6:5 they matched "strength" with body and both "heart" and "soul" with the spirit which decides and wills. What they missed was a mental aspect. So they supplied it.

It was clear to readers of all eras what Deuteronomy 6:5 meant by "with all your heart, and with all your soul, and with all your might." The point of Deuteronomy 6:5 was not to distinguish functions or organs or capacities, but rather to cover all the inner resources that a person could have and to think of them as a whole. What is required is to love God completely and without reservation. The emphasis belongs on the repeated "all." The word "all" produces the spiritual intensity and concentration in this part of the Shema that the word translated "one" or "only" or "alone" did in the first part.

Our excursion through Deuteronomy 6:4-5 is finished. All that remains is to note that, although we have inspected each part separately, the Shema is an integrated whole. The confession of faith is the basis for the commandment and the whole is tied together by the intensifying words for completeness. It works like this: Because we know that only God is God (Deuteronomy 6:4), we acknowledge that only a total response is adequate (Deuteronomy 6:5).

The second part of Jesus' commandment is "You shall love your neighbor as yourself." The quotation is from Leviticus 19:18. What can we say about this verse in itself? The whole of Leviticus 19 is a series of commandments about living a life of holiness. The title of the chapter and its thesis are in verse 2: "You shall be holy; for I the LORD your God am holy." The commandments and explanations which follow constitute the recipe for a holy life, a life corresponding to the nature of God. We saw in Deuteronomy 7:8-9 that the command to love God was also a command to live in a way corresponding to the nature of God. The chapter is punctuated at verse 18 and again at verse 34 by the sentence "You shall love your neighbor as yourself."

In verse 18 the neighbor is a fellow citizen, as the adjoining verse shows:

> You shall not hate your brother in your heart, but you shall reason with your neighbor, lest you bear sin because of him. You shall not take vengeance or bear any grudge against the sons of your own people, but you shall love your neighbor as yourself (Leviticus 19:17-18).

By contrast, in verse 34 the neighbor is a resident alien.

> When a stranger sojourns with you in your land, you shall not do him wrong. The stranger who sojourns with you shall be to you as the native among you,

and you shall love him as yourself; for you were strangers in the land of Egypt (Leviticus 19:33-34).

We can see that the neighbor is defined neither by family nor ethnic ties, nor yet by a common religious affiliation. Family, ethnic and religious ties would fit verse 18 but not verse 34. Rather, the neighbor is defined by social ties resulting from living in the same vicinity. There is no mention, however, of social hierarchy. My neighbor is the butcher, the baker, the candlestick-maker, the person I meet in the ordinary course of my life, whether that person is friendly or hostile, recent immigrant or old settler, boss or employee. The references to citizens (verse 18) and noncitizens (verse 34) covers everybody.

The passages we have quoted should tell us not only who is meant by neighbor but what it means to love that neighbor. In verses 17-18 the opposite of loving is "hating in your heart," "taking vengeance," and "bearing a grudge," while in verses 33-34 the opposite of loving is "doing a wrong." Two of the four items are social, while hating and bearing grudges take place at the wellsprings of action. Any definition of loving the neighbor must include both outward acts and inner motivations. The meaning of love is shown in the phrases "reason with your neighbor" and "the stranger shall be to you as the native among you." Reasoning, of course, does not imply that the misguided neighbor is to be approved of but that persuasion, not violence, is to be the cure for the wrongheadedness. Any definition of loving the neighbor must include treating even the most pigheaded with both respect and equity.

Our excursion through the commandment "You shall love your neighbor as yourself" would not be complete without asking what "as yourself" contributes to the whole. Most modern interpretations that I have heard say, "Well, first you have to love yourself." Let's stop right there. I don't see anything in any place Leviticus 19:18 is quoted that commands self-love. At most, Leviticus 19:18 presupposes that I will, of course, look after my own interests. What it commands is that I exercise as much care over other people's interests as I do over my own. In any event, Leviticus 19:18 does not promote assertiveness training and exercises in self-improvement and mental health.

Let's look at Leviticus 19 to see if it gives us a clue to the way "as yourself" works in relation to the command to love the neighbor. Verse 34 is quite explicit. "The stranger...shall be as the native...for you were strangers in the land of Egypt." This means, to paraphrase the verse, that out of your own collective historic experience as a stranger you will know how to treat strangers rightly. What does "as yourself" mean? "As yourself" means cultivating a long and accurate memory. "As yourself" means using that memory to aid the act of imagination by which you see things from someone else's point of view. "As yourself" means relying upon past experience as a guide to action. We ought to note that verse 34 doesn't authorize just any random past experience as a guide to action. Rather, it authorizes a collective experience of a large group of people, an experience which had been analyzed in all of its aspects from all possible points of view and which was formative of the identity of Israel. This experience, it should be noted, was basically a bad trip, a bitter period of suffering as victims of oppression and slavery.

We pause here on our tour through the world of Leviticus 19:18 and 34 to ask what, in the world of the modern Christian, would correspond to, or even vaguely resemble, slavery in Egypt. What shared experiences are bad enough and universal enough? Older readers of this book may recall World War II or the Great Depression or the Civil Rights Movement. All readers will share experiences, personal or vicarious, of death and dying. In addition to these are the tough times of our common history, which we can enter through books and imagination, experiences such as the Civil War or the rigors of pioneer life or the destruction of Native American cultures, or the dislocations of the Industrial Revolution. Here's another idea, a very simple one. Let's adopt the experience of Israel in Egypt as our own, entering into it imaginatively, and grasping from the inside, as it were, the alienation and oppression of the victims.

Our excursion through the command to love one's neighbor as oneself is finished. We have seen that the command is to treat with respect and equity all those with whom we deal. The criterion for so treating them is seeing the world from their point of view on the basis of our own past experience of oppression. It is this commandment which Jesus added to the Shema to form a double command of love.

Question #3: The third of the questions raised at the beginning of this chapter was: *What kind of interpretive act is it to put two verses together?* What do they do to influence each other? To answer this question, our tour of the world of the love commandment returns to the time of Jesus and the situation of his first audience. The first task is to place the two passages close together, as Jesus did, so the meaning of one can spill over to the other. Here they are:

Hear, O Israel: The LORD our God is one LORD; and you shall love the LORD your God with all your heart, and with all your soul, and with all your might. . . . You shall love your neighbor as yourself (Deuteronomy 6:4-5; Leviticus 19:18).

Now that we can see them together, we can say that the cumulative effect is an enormous heightening of emphasis on the word "love." Repeating the word a second time has made it stand out from the other words. It is no accident that Christians have thought "love" to be their most important obligation and have organized much thought, formal and informal, around this term. The fact is, Jesus set us up for it when he put these two passages together.

The commandment about love for neighbor takes on new meaning when it is set next to the Shema, a meaning which spills over from the Shema. To begin with, it is rescued from obscurity in the midst of a chapter about holiness. By the time of Jesus, Leviticus 19:18 surely had long since been detached from its context in Leviticus 19 and circulated as an independent teaching. We ought not to credit Jesus with isolating it; what Jesus did was to give it a new context. Leviticus 19:18 had already lost its basis in the holiness of God. It now acquired a new basis in the unity of God. It makes a special kind of sense when Jesus relates it to the unity of God. Because God is integrated and unified in will and action, we can't live our own lives with two standards, one for ourselves and our friends, the other for people outside our circle.

The other meaning which spills over from the Shema to Leviticus 19:18 may be called religious intensity. As we have seen, the repeated emphasis on "all" in "with all your heart and with all your soul," together with the direct address "Hear, O Israel" and the little word translated "one" or "only" or "alone," gave the Shema a religious intensity. Here we need to see that the religious intensity of the Shema rescues Leviticus 19:18 from any danger of becoming a piece of prudential advice to use persuasion rather than feuds in the manner of the Hatfields and McCoys. If many Christians have an almost mystical sense of the neighbor, it is only because Jesus has set us up to view Leviticus 19:18 with considerable religious intensity.

The Shema also takes on new meaning from its association with Leviticus 19:18. To begin with, the social dimensions of loving God are emphasized. There is something about religious intensity that tends to focus on God alone and to neglect everything else. Bringing what is easy to neglect into focus without losing the primary focus is quite a trick, as every photographer knows. Yet that is what happens here. The first new meaning the Shema acquires is a restoration of its social dimensions.

The second alteration in the meaning of the Shema which occurs when it is set next to Leviticus 19:18 is an unfortunate one, I think. When the two commandments are set next to each other, their character as command is emphasized. The repetition of "you *shall*" de-emphasizes the statement of the unity and integrity of God which is the basis of the command. We focus on what is commanded and pay less attention to the God who alone has any business issuing these commands. You may have noticed that Matthew and Luke don't quote the first part of the Shema. One reason they neglect it is, of course, that the Shema begins with a personal address of Israel and "Israel" isn't the name of the people for whom they are writing. The other reason Matthew and Luke dropped the first part of the Shema was that they didn't think of it as an important part of the commandment. They were thinking in terms of what is commanded rather that in terms of responding to the one God.

Question #4: We come, finally, to the last of the questions with which we began the chapter. *What does his giving great importance to the love commandment tell us about Jesus' relation to the debates about the Old Testament law?*

The importance Jesus gives to the love commandment is phrased differently in each Gospel. We can place the question asked, and the answer about the importance of the love commandment, in a table.

Matthew 22:36,38-39	Mark 12:28,31	Luke 10:25,28
Which is the great commandment in the law?	Which commandment is the first of all?	What shall I do to inherit eternal life?
This is the great and first commandment. And a second is like it.	There is no other commandment greater than these.	Do this, and you will live.

Matthew and Mark both use the term "first" and the term "great" or "greater." Luke doesn't use either term, but his questioner asks about the greatest and most important of all possible questions—salvation. In all three cases, however, it is clear that Jesus has given the love commandment a special place in his own teaching and a special place in Old Testament law.

A learned debate about Old Testament law was a principal ingredient of the intellectual environment of Jesus' time. It was as common as discussions of child-rearing or education are today, and it took place on as many levels. In the Gospels we can see Jesus participating in that debate in both town and countryside, with common folk and intellectuals. Here are some examples. After Jesus' disciples plucked grain on the sabbath, Jesus concluded a dispute with the Pharisees by saying, "The sabbath was made for man, not man for the sabbath; so the Son of man is lord even of the sabbath" (Mark 2:27-28). Mark 7:1-23 contains a lengthy dispute over the status of dietary laws and ritual cleanliness; Mark 11:27—12:34 contains a long series of discussions, mostly disputes, over the law.

One part of the discussion about the law concerned the love commandment. We can see some of this discussion in documents called the *Testaments of the Twelve Patriarchs*, written over a period of years beginning before Jesus' time and ending afterward. The testaments are based on the blessing which the dying Jacob gave his assembled sons in Genesis 49. Each testament is a lengthy affair incorporating religious and ethical thinking and admonition current at approximately the time of Jesus. Much of it is mulling over bits of the Old Testament including, every now and then, the love commandment. Here are a few examples.

> Keep, therefore, my children, the law of God,
> And get singleness,
> And walk in guilelessness
> Not playing the busybody with the business of
>   your neighbor
> But love the Lord and your neighbor
> Have compassion on the poor and the weak.
>   (T. Issachar 5:1-2)
> I loved the Lord;
> Likewise also every man with all my heart.
>   (T. Issachar 7:6)
> Love the Lord through all your life
> And one another with a true heart.
>   (T. Dan 5:3)

If I had not already said that these passages were from a Jewish document, you might have guessed they were from some early Christian piece. Now you may begin to wonder whether Jesus had read one or more of the Testaments or whether the authors of the Testaments stole Jesus' ideas. Both possibilities have been raised. However, I think these two are not the only alternatives, and I also feel they both miss the significance of the use of the love commandment. The real significance of the use of the love commandment in the Testaments is that it was a well-known and much-approved element of moral discourse. That means that when Jesus commended Deuteronomy 6:5

and Leviticus 19:18, he wasn't proposing something new. Rather, he was taking part in a larger discussion of the law.

Another part of the discussion about the law concerned First Principles. This discussion had been going on for several hundred years by the time of Jesus. Here is a quotation from long before Jesus' time:

> Afterward [wisdom] appeared on earth and lived among men. She is the book of the commandments of God. (Baruch 3:37—4:1)

This quotation shows that the Jewish discussion really did think of intellectual, moral, and legal principles which are First Principles, corresponding to and participating in the structure of the universe and everything in it. Here Wisdom, the structure of the universe, lives among us as a book. To put it another way, what is in the Bible is what makes the universe tick. The big argument in the Judaism of Jesus' day was whether any one verse in "the book of the commandments of God" was more fundamental than the rest.

Most people agreed that it was possible to summarize the law in the sense of making one verse into a mental chapter heading and mentally grouping others beneath it as applications of the principle. One set of Hebrew terms used an analogy from genealogy to describe this intellectual procedure: The general principles were called "ancestors"; individual cases were called "descendants." Here is an example from a century after Jesus:

> Rabbi Akiba said, "'Thou shalt love thy neighbor as thyself'; this is the greatest general principle in the Torah." (Sifra Leviticus 19:18)

Rabbi Akiba used part of the love commandment to organize a substantial segment of the verses of the Old Testament. For him it was the greatest of the "ancestors."

The second position went beyond the first. This alternative position regarded the basic concepts in the Old Testament as the substance of the law. The genealogical analogy was not very important to them. They did not think the *words* of the Bible corresponded to the structure of the universe. It was, rather, the fundamental *ideas* of the Bible, its intellectual structures, which corresponded to the fundamental ideas which are the structure of the universe. Philo of Alexandria, who lived at approximately the same time as Jesus but quite far away, was one such person. Here is what he says about law in the Old Testament:

> But among the vast number of particular truths and principles there studied, there stand out practically high above the others two heads: one of duty to God as shown by piety and holiness, one of duty to men as shown by humanity and justice. (Spec. Leg. 2.63)

In other places Philo identifies the Ten Commandments as "head" laws; here he identifies "duty to God" and "duty to men" as "head" laws. Clearly, it's the idea that counts, not the wording. I believe Philo would have commended Jesus' choice of Deuteronomy 6:5 to state one's duty to God and Leviticus 19:18 to express one's duty to others.

To which camp did Jesus belong? When he stressed the importance of Deuteronomy 6:5 and Leviticus 19:18, was he making them "ancestors," using them like Rabbi Akiba used Leviticus 19:18? Or was he putting the love principle at the center of the moral universe as Philo might have? Most of his followers thought he was more like Philo; some thought he was more like a rabbi. Since all the quotations we have from rabbis come from after Jesus' time, it is also possible that in Jesus' day the boundaries between the alternative positions were not nearly as sharp as they were later. Perhaps in Jesus' day one didn't have to choose sides because the discussion was more free-form, the options more open.

It seems clear that Jesus was an active participant in the debate going on around him about Old Testament law, even if we don't know quite where he fits in. The chances are you'll be on the right track if you think that Jesus broke the categories of the discussion about law even while he participated in it. It's the sort of thing you'd expect from Jesus. And Jesus' followers thought the love commandment was important, not only because Jesus said it but because they saw in Jesus' ministry, in his self-giving death and in his resurrection, what love means. They interpreted not only what was said but the one who said it. The Jesus who put Deuteronomy 6:5 and Leviticus 19:18 together and gave them great importance was the same Jesus who loved God with all his heart, soul, mind, and strength and who loved his neighbor as himself.

3

Mark's Interpretation

In the last chapter we inspected the achievement of Jesus himself. To do this we looked at the New Testament, trying to see, through the window of the stories in the New Testament, the figure of Jesus. There are times when windows are foggy and other times when you look out a window and see your own reflection: sometimes you have to strain to see *through* the windows. We have been quite fortunate in the case of the love commandment. The New Testament stories about the love commandment are reasonably transparent to the historical Jesus. We have had no trouble seeing that Jesus put together Deuteronomy 6:5 and Leviticus 19:18 and gave great importance to them.

In this chapter and the four which follow it we will inspect the earliest interpretations of Jesus, the ones in the New Testament. We will not look *through* the stories but *at* them. You could think of this as a study of windows. The focus of our interest in these chapters is not Jesus himself but the portrait of Jesus done by various early interpreters.

I use the term portrait to make it clear what kind of stories we have in the New Testament. Near the end of the Gospel of John we find a passage which tells how the literary portraits were written and why:

> Now Jesus did many other signs in the presence of the disciples, which are not written in this book; but these are written that you may believe that Jesus is the Christ, the Son of God, and that believing you may have life in his name.
> (John 20:30-31)

These verses say something about how Gospels were composed. Here we don't have the diary of some companion of Jesus, with daily entries about events in the order in which they occurred; rather, we have works organized artistically to show Jesus in his proper light. The ordering isn't accidental; the details are not random. A mind is at work in the composing of each portrait of Jesus. The result is more like an Ansel Adams portfolio of Yosemite than like the photo album of a trip to Yosemite I might compile with my trusty instamatic.

The quotation from the Gospel of John also tells us something about why the Gospels were written. These are no reports of bystanders, no neutral accounts. The writers who composed the portraits of Jesus shared the basic conviction that Jesus was raised from the dead. Everything in the New Testament was written by Christians; everything is written from faith and for faith. The New Testament, that is to say, is blatantly biased. It wants you to believe that Jesus is the Christ, the Son of God. Mark even uses as the title of his Gospel, "The Gospel of Jesus Christ, the Son of God" (Mark 1:1).

We know much less about when and where Gospels were written than about how and why they were written. Most scholars date the book of Mark, the earliest of the Gospels, to about A.D. 70 and consider any location at the eastern end of the Mediterranean a possible place of composition. Mark was written by and for a specific group of Christians more than a third of a century after the events it narrates.

During the period before Mark, stories about Jesus were told again and again. They were grouped together, shaped to fit church contexts, applied to church problems, linked together in various ways, given introductions and conclusions. The storytelling took place in gatherings of Christians where Jesus' presence was deeply felt. In this context some Christians had dreams and revelations about Jesus. After a while it was hard to know the difference between a story about Jesus told in the light of his crucifixion and resurrection, and a story about the risen Christ seen in a dream. When that time came, it was time to get a Gospel on paper.

Mapping Mark's Gospel

It has been said, only partly as a joke, that the Gospel of Mark is a Passion narrative with a long introduction. The truth of that claim is that the Gospel of Mark rushes to a climax at the cross. There is little tendency to linger over individual stories, dwelling lovingly on this aspect or that. No sooner is a story begun than it is finished and Jesus is rushing on to the next event. The author hurries us along by using the word translated "immediately" or "at once" over and over (eleven times in chapter 1 alone!) and by keeping his stories short and snappy. Predictions of the crucifixion and resurrection are planted at the right places (8:31-33; 9:30-32; 10:32-34) to draw our attention toward the end of the story. The author is in a hurry to get us to the story of the crucifixion and resurrection. Once we have those stories straight, Mark appears to think we will be equipped to understand the rest.

Mark puts the story of the love commandment in the week which ended with the crucifixion and resurrection, so we need to look at the passages which tell about that last climactic week. Here is a bare-bones outline:

11:1-26	Jesus Takes Charge
11:27—12:44	Public Teaching and Controversy
13:1-37	Private Teaching
14:1—16:8	Passion Narrative

The first section, which I called "Jesus Takes Charge," contains the story of the entry into Jerusalem; the story of the termination of commerce in sacrificial animals, which is sometimes called the cleansing of the temple; and a strange story about cursing a fig tree. In the first story Jesus takes charge of the city as its king; in the second Jesus takes charge of the temple; and in the third Jesus takes charge of nature. In each case, it should be said, Jesus "takes charge" in some strange, symbolic way, some way that wasn't quite public, or that wasn't acknowledged by everyone around as honest-to-goodness "taking charge."

The second section, from Mark 11:27 to the end of chapter 12, contains four exchanges with persons of various parties and professional groups, plus some teaching at the end. I have called this *Public* Teaching and Controversy because of the public location, "as he was walking in the temple" (Mark 11:27). Jesus and his followers are in a public area of the temple complex, strolling along an arcade in the midst of the holiday crowd. By the way of contrast, I have called the third section *Private* Teaching because of the way the request is made, "Peter and James and John and Andrew asked him privately" (Mark 13:3). The four exchanges in section 2 are these:
1. 11:27—12:13. Controversy with chief priests, scribes, and elders over Jesus' authority, including the story of the vineyard.
2. 12:13-17. Controversy with Pharisees and Herodians about paying taxes to Caesar.
3. 12:18-27. Controversy with Sadducees over the resurrection.
4. 12:28-34. Discussion with a scribe about the law.

The fourth exchange is the story of the love commandment. We notice something about the quality of the exchanges which distinguishes the fourth exchange from the preceding three. The first three are controversies Mark says are designed to trick Jesus or trap him in some way. In the first exchange, the attack is a frontal one, "By what authority. . .?" (Mark 11:28). In the second exchange, some people were sent "to entrap him in his talk" (Mark 12:13). These same people appeared earlier in Mark's story as Jesus' first really threatening opponents, "The Pharisees went out, and immediately held counsel with the Herodians against him, how to destroy him" (Mark 3:6). In the third exchange, the Sadducees, "who say that there is no resurrection" (Mark 12:18), ask about the legal implications of resurrection, surely a case of "Don't confuse me with facts; my mind is made up."

But the fourth exchange is not a controversy at all. Here the scribe asks, not because he wants to trick Jesus or trap him, but because he saw "that he answered them well" (Mark 12:28). Clearly, Mark wants us to see Jesus dealing with all the categories of important people in the Jewish society of his day. Most of them are hostile, though the first group orchestrates the confrontation. In each of the first three exchanges, Jesus deals with groups: the chief priests, scribes, and elders appear as a group in 11:27 and argue among themselves in 11:31-32; the second delegation consists of "some of the Pharisees and some of the Herodians" in 12:13; the Sadducees appear in a body in 12:17. Only in the final exchange about the love commandment does a single person, "one of the scribes" (Mark 12:28), appear.

We need to pause here on our tour through the world of the love commandment to look back at where we have been and to make sure we know where we are. We have looked at Mark's portrait of Jesus' public teaching during the final week, as found in Mark 11:27--12:44. We have seen that Mark carefully places Jesus in four encounters with important people, three with hostile groups and one with an individual who is not at all hostile. We have had occasion to observe Mark's literary craftsmanship. Now we need to consider briefly the story of the love commandment Mark inherited from the Christian store of stories about Jesus. Did Mark know a dialogue about the love commandment, or was it a controversy? The answer, I think, is that Mark knew a dialogue. Consider this argument. What if Mark knew a dialogue? It would have been easy and convenient for Mark to turn a dialogue about the love commandment into a story of controversy. If he had done so, he would have had a tidy, symmetrical series of four controversies. What would be different if Mark knew a controversy? If he had known the story of the love commandment as a controversy, Mark would have had no motivation to change it into a dialogue. This is the argument: The fact that we have a dialogue about the love commandment in this particular place in Mark's Gospel and not a controversy means that Mark knew a dialogue and did not alter the form. Let me state the conclusion another way. We are dealing with a story which is pre-Markan in form as well as substance. Mark has set it in a literary context in the final public ministry of Jesus in the temple at Jerusalem, like a jewel in a crown. But he has passed it along in just the form in which he found it.

A Dialogue about God

We are ready to turn now to the story of the love commandment Mark knew and told.

> And one of the scribes came up and heard them disputing with one another, and seeing that he answered them well, asked him, "Which commandment is the first of all?" Jesus answered, "The first is, 'Hear, O Israel: The Lord our God, the Lord is one; and you shall love the Lord your God with all your heart, and with all your soul, and with all your mind, and with all your strength.' The second is this, 'You shall love your neighbor as yourself.' There is no other commandment greater than these." And the scribe said to him, "You are right, Teacher; you have truly said that he is one, and there is no other but he; and to love him with all the heart, and with all the understanding, and with all the strength, and to love one's neighbor as oneself, is much more than all whole burnt offerings and sacrifices." And when Jesus saw that he answered wisely, he said to him, "You are not far from the kingdom of God." And after that no one dared to ask him any question (Mark 12:28-34).

The story line is very simple, a dialogue with two speeches for each participant. Here is the outline.

1. Scribe asks question.
2. Jesus answers.
3. Scribe paraphrases answer.
4. Jesus approves.

We will take up each of the four parts of the outline in turn.

1. The first part includes phrases which connect this dialogue to the controversies which precede it. The scribe is pictured as someone passing along in the crowd, milling about the public areas of the temple. This scribe isn't part of the conspiracy against Jesus. He is an independent passerby. He hears Jesus teaching and fielding questions. He makes the independent judgment that Jesus is doing a good job. So he decides to join the conversation.

The first observation we need to make in our tour of the world of this story has to do with the category of scribe. Scribes were professional Jewish thinkers, resident intellectuals, people who drew up learned opinions on matters of Old Testament law. Some scribes were Pharisees, some Sadducees; some were born into priestly families, some not. The category is a professional one, not an ideological one.

The Greek term, translated "scribe" here, could also be translated "secretary" or "clerk." It was a widely-used term, as widely used as our term "secretary," and with as wide a range of meanings. Each time in antiquity a committee was formed a secretary was elected, as many inscriptions from every city in the ancient world show. When Paul and some companions get into trouble in Ephesus, as related in Acts 19, someone makes a persuasive speech to calm the mob. Who is that someone? He is called "the town clerk" in the RSV (Acts 19:35), but the Greek term is the same as the one translated "scribe" in our story.

The point of this discussion is that while the professional category "scribe" belongs to Jewish society and not to the larger non-Jewish world, the word for such Jewish professionals was used to mean something different in the wider world. If Mark had wanted to be understood by readers who knew little about what certain Jewish professionals were called, he would have used a different word. That he used "scribe" as the term for this professional class shows he didn't *choose* the word. Rather, the word was part of the story he knew. Like the substance of the story and the dialogue form of the story, the term "scribe" takes us to the Palestinian Jewish environment in which the story was told.

The second observation we need to make about the setting is that the scribe thinks he has arrived at a debating society. Jesus, as the scribe perceives him, is an intellectual, setting forth an intellectual position to which other intellectuals respond with counterarguments, challenges to premises and presuppositions, and questions of application and scope. He judges Jesus here on the quality of his answers—"he answered them well"—and later will judge Jesus on the coherence of the position itself.

The intellectual atmosphere and social arrangement that the scribe presumes was a familiar one to city people of his day. Philosophers of various types often held forth on street corners or in public areas of temples or under the great colonnaded porches of the market squares. Some people were full-time disciples of a given philosopher; others shopped around; a great many more paused to listen for a while as they went about their business. The author of Acts shows Paul as an active participant in this urban intellectual environment when he visits Athens:

> So he argued . . . in the market place every day with those who chanced to be there. Some also of the Epicurean and Stoic philosophers met him. . . . Now all the Athenians and the foreigners who lived there spent their time in nothing except telling or hearing something new (Acts 17:17,18,21).

The author of Acts is poking fun at the Athenians' quest for intellectual fads and trivia while he sets the scene for Paul's speech on the Areopagus. He can afford to poke fun because everyone who read his words knew about the settings in which the intellectual life of antiquity took place. Mark and his first readers knew such settings too. So did the early Palestinian Christians who passed on this story about Jesus. It is such a setting which the scribe presumes.

Our final observation should be about the scribe's question, "Which commandment is the first of all?" (Mark 12:28). It is not a trick question or a trap. Rather, it is a serious question that probes for the foundation on which Jesus' whole intellectual position rests. It is a Jewish question, presuming that any intellectual position will have the Old Testament law as its foundation.

What does the question mean? We know nothing except what the story tells us. The only possible clue in the question is the word "of all." What does the scribe mean by using "of all"? Is he asking "Which commandment is (the) first (ancestor) of all (the other commandments)?" in the manner of Rabbi Akiba a century later? or is he asking "Which commandment is (the Old Testament's way of expressing the principle which is) first of all (constituents of reality)?" in the manner of Philo? The question is deliberately open-ended. The scribe waits for Jesus' answer.

2. Our tour of the world of the love commandment moves on to the second part of the dialogue that is Mark's story: Jesus' answer. We looked at Jesus' answer rather carefully in chapter 2. Here we need only recall that discussion. Having been asked for a single commandment, Jesus gives two. He even numbers them, "The first is. . . .The second is this. . ." (Mark 12:30-31). He quotes Deuteronomy 6:4-5, the Shema. He quotes Leviticus 19:18. And he rounds off his answer by linking the two together, "There is no other commandment greater than these" (Mark 12:31).

What is it in this answer which the scribe finds so exciting? We know he approves wholeheartedly. What is it that triggers his approval? I think what got the scribe all excited was the addition of the fourth phrase "with all your mind" to the three in the Old Testament. The mental aspect of love and the corresponding mental-ness in the picture of God is what appealed to him. We will have to test my answer against the specifics of the scribe's response.

3. The third part of the dialogue about the love commandment is a speech by the scribe. He paraphrases Jesus' answer to his question, enthusiastically emphasizing some phrases and limiting or applying the whole.

The first observation we need to make is how the scribe treats Jesus. His approving evaluation, "You are right, Teacher; you have truly said. . ." is remarkably collegial, claiming an equality with Jesus as a fellow-intellectual, a soul-mate sharing a particular theological passion, a senior member of the same academic stream.

Our second observation about the scribe's reply to Jesus is that it concerns God. The scribe's primary response is to the quotation of Deuteronomy 6:4, "the Lord our God, the Lord is one." He paraphrases the statement to bring out its meaning. It is a statement of the unity of God, "he is one." He then defines unity by a statement of the incomparability of God, "there is no other but he." Notice that the scribe, following Jewish custom, doesn't say the name God. The problem of the one and the many was much discussed in ancient philosophy, and philosophically-inclined Jews like the scribe in our story joined the discussion with enthusiasm. The scribe thinks that Jesus is altogether correct in placing the unity of God as the foundation of his intellectual system and at the foundation of reality itself.

Paul participated in the same discussion as Jesus and the scribe, and so did his philosophically-oriented Gentile converts in Corinth. Paul wrote to them, quoting their own phrases, "We know that 'an idol has no real existence' and that 'there is no God but one'" (1 Corinthians 8:4). Paul's converts drew the wrong conclusions, to be sure, and Paul wrote his letter to set them straight. But he agreed with their basic premises.

Our third observation about the scribe's reply to Jesus is to call attention to his stress on the mental aspect of loving God. I suggested earlier that it was this which triggered his enthusiastic response. We have already seen that the scribe links Jesus to a wide-ranging philosophical discussion. Here we need to note specifically that in his paraphrase of Deuteronomy 6:5 the scribe uses one phrase that is different from the one used by Jesus. Instead of saying "with all your mind," he says "with all the understanding," using a different Greek word, one with a more philosophical tone. The effect of the use of a different phrase is to call attention to the mental aspect of loving God.

Our final observation about the scribe's reply to Jesus concerns his rejection of sacrifice. Mark places this story in the temple so that we can see the scribe dismiss the whole of the activity around him with a wave of his hand while he judges obedience to the love commandment to be "much more than all whole burnt offerings and sacrifices." The scribe takes his clues to right worship from another set of Old Testament passages than those which command sacrifices. He may have had one of these passages in mind:

> Has the LORD as great delight in burnt offerings and sacrifices,
>   as in obeying the voice of the LORD?
> Behold, to obey is better than sacrifice,
>   and to hearken than the fat of rams. (1 Samuel 15:22)
>
> For I desire steadfast love and not sacrifice,
>   the knowledge of God, rather than burnt offerings. (Hosea 6:6)

Passages which urge love rather than sacrifice appealed to at least two groups of people. First, there were those who lived much too far from Jerusalem to engage in sacrifice but who understood their own worship and service of God to be authentic and first-rate, deficient in no respect. This group included Greek-speaking Jews living all over the Mediterranean world. And then there was a second group of people whose ideas of God didn't include God's appreciation of animal sacrifice. According to their way of thinking, only the unsophisticated think God likes to taste or smell an offering. If God is characterized by unity or incomparability, surely the only worship which is appropriate takes place as an inner movement of the deep secret sources of human thought and action. Such a person is our scribe. I'm sure he never heard the sentence "God is spirit, and those who worship him must worship in spirit and truth" (John 4:24). But if he had heard it, he would have been very pleased. He would think it expressed his own point of view very well and that it agreed with the Teacher who quoted Deuteronomy 6:4-5 and Leviticus 19:18 as the commandments which are first of all.

4. The last section of Mark's dialogue about the love commandment is Jesus' final reply. Actually, this section of the dialogue has three components and we will take them up in turn.

Before Jesus' reply to the scribe there is a remark, "when Jesus saw that he answered wisely." This phrase is the storyteller's way of taking the audience inside Jesus' head. The storyteller informs us what Jesus observes and what motivates his reply. The clue to what he observes is the term translated "wisely," a philosophical term for appropriate responses. Jesus observes that the scribe has grasped correctly the philosophical import of his use of Deuteronomy 6:4-5 and Leviticus 19:18. That is why he approves the scribe's response.

Jesus' reply, "You are not far from the kingdom of God," affirms the scribe and partially confirms the correctness of his interpretation of Jesus' answer to his question. Jesus uses his own favorite phrase, "The kingdom of God." Mark first introduces the phrase in a summary of Jesus' characteristic message at the beginning of his Gospel: "Jesus came into Galilee, preaching the gospel of God, and saying, 'The time is fulfilled, and the kingdom of God is at hand; repent, and believe in the gospel'" (Mark 1:14-15). Jesus announces the reign of God and invites belief in it. It seems to me that it is the scribe's passionate and single-minded focus on *God* that corresponds to Jesus' characteristic message. His concentration and intensity, his radical downgrading of everything which distracts from loving God, are what repenting and believing mean. His exclusive attention to God alone is what the kingdom of God and the gospel of God is all about.

How shall we interpret "not far"? If Jesus approves of the scribe's single-mindedness, why doesn't he say "You are already a citizen of God's kingdom, already subject to God's sovereign rule"? Why does he hold back, qualifying his approval? Interpreters often suggest that the scribe has the words right but now must put love into practice. That interpretation doesn't satisfy me. The scribe has shrugged off the animal sacrifice which his contemporaries took to be an adequate practice of the love of God, and I see no hint that either he or Jesus is thinking about any substitute practice. Let me suggest an alternative interpretation of "not far," one which has the advantage of staying within the range of what the story has dealt with so far. I propose that Jesus has reservations about paraphrasing his answer in philosophical categories accessible only to the intellectual elite. Notice how careful the storyteller is about the kind of language each person in this dialogue uses. Jesus uses his own phrase, "the kingdom of God," and quotes the Old Testament. It's a kind of "just folks" vocabulary and approach to communication. The scribe's vocabulary and general use of language are quite different. Two quotes about the unity and incomparability of God drawn from Hellenistic-Jewish

39

philosophy come to his mind, as does a fancy alternative term for the mental faculty. He is an intellectual and uses language appropriate to his status. I am suggesting that "not far" implies a criticism by Jesus of the scribe's elitism, not because the paraphrase is inadequate to the content, but rather because the paraphrase is insufficient to the mission. The scribe's paraphrase validly interprets Jesus to the scribe himself and to a few others; Jesus' message is for all people.

The Final Sentence

"After that no one dared to ask him any question" is Mark's conclusion to all four exchanges Jesus had while walking in the temple, 11:27—12:34. It is an appropriate conclusion to the three hostile exchanges, where it means that Jesus was so good at seeing through trick questions that the hostile questioners gave up to avoid further embarrassment. It is a less satisfactory conclusion to the story of the love commandment, where, having been approved, the scribe should feel encouraged to ask follow-up questions.

Our tour of the world of the dialogue about the love commandment in the Gospel of Mark is finished. We have located Mark's story on the map of the Gospel and seen how it fits into its literary context. We have examined the parts of the dialogue in turn. In the process we have discovered that Mark's story is one which he received from some anonymous Christian storyteller. This earliest form of the love commandment is Mark's interpretation of a storyteller's interpretation of Jesus' interpretation of two verses from the Old Testament. As far as the eye can see, it's all interpretation, "elephants all the way down." How clearly are we seeing the historical Jesus in the portraiture Mark presents to us? I think we glimpse Jesus as he really lived very clearly indeed. I think that Jesus' own contemporaries, like the scribe in the story, were most strongly impressed by the intensity of his concentration on God alone.

4

Matthew's Interpretation

Matthew's story about the love commandment is so different from Mark's that it is hard to imagine Matthew had Mark's text before him when he wrote. Let's place the stories side by side to compare them.

Matthew 22:34-40
34-35. But when the Pharisees heard that he had silenced the Sadducees, they came together. And one of them, a lawyer, asked him a question, to test him.
36. "Teacher, which is the great commandment in the law?"
37. And he said to him,

"'You shall love the Lord your God with all your heart, and with all your soul, and with all your mind.'

38. This is the great and first commandment. 39. And a second is like it,

Mark 12:28-34
28. And one of the scribes came up and heard them disputing with one another, and seeing that he answered them well, asked him,

"Which commandment is the first of all?"
29. Jesus answered, "The first is, 'Hear, O Israel: The Lord our God, the Lord is one;
30. and you shall love the Lord your God with all your heart, and with all your soul, and with all your mind, and with all your strength.'
31. The second is this,

'You shall love your neighbor as yourself.'
40. On these two commandments depend all the law and the prophets."

'You shall love your neighbor as yourself.' There is no other commandment greater than these."

32-33. And the scribe said to him, "You are right, Teacher; you have truly said that he is one, and there is no other but he; and to love him with all the heart, and with all the understanding, and with all the strength, and to love one's neighbor as oneself, is much more than all whole burnt offerings and sacrifices."

34. And when Jesus saw that he answered wisely, he said to him, "You are not far from the kingdom of God." And after that no one dared to ask him any question.

The first differences between Matthew and Mark are in the first verses. Matthew has a lawyer ask a trick question; Mark has a scribe ask a serious question which contains no trick. The questions they ask are substantially the same. The only difference between the answers is that Mark shows Jesus quoting the Shema in its entirety; Matthew shows him quoting only Deuteronomy 6:5. The big difference is the way the stories end. Both endings say what the love commandment means. Matthew shows Jesus saying what the love commandment means: it has to do with interpreting Scripture. Mark has the scribe say what the love commandment means: it has to do with worship, as we saw in chapter 3. Another difference between Matthew and Mark is that Matthew has a single question and a single answer whereas Mark has each person speak twice.

We all need to be careful to leave a "trail of bread crumbs" along the route of our tour through the world of Matthew's story, because we are dealing not just with one story, Matthew's, but with two, Matthew's and Mark's, in comparison. It would be easy to get lost while exploring a multiple text, one of which is an interpretation of an interpretation.

Mapping Matthew's Gospel

Let's take up first the setting of the story, its location in the Gospel. Mark, we remember, put it during the last week of Jesus' ministry, at the end of a series of encounters in a public area of the temple in Jerusalem. Matthew follows Mark but inserts more stories into Mark's outline. Here is an outline of the relevant section of the story.

| Matthew 21:1-22 | Mark 11:1-26 | Jesus Takes Charge |
| Matthew 21:23—23:39 | Mark 11:27—12:44 | Public Teaching and Controversy |

Matthew has rearranged Mark's outline, in the section I have called "Jesus Takes Charge," in order to put the story of the fig tree all together instead of splitting it into two paragraphs, as Mark does. Presumably he thinks this makes a more rational and coherent narrative. In the section of public teaching there are more extensive changes. Matthew inserts three sections into Mark's outline, expands one section enormously, and omits one. Despite the changes, Mark's basic outline remains clear and most of Mark's material is copied out word for word. The three controversies that we found in Mark appear exactly the same in Matthew. Then comes the story of the love commandment, in exactly the same place in the outline as in Mark. The story is recognizable, but the differences are substantial and significant. Our tour of the world of the love commandment moves in closer to the passage now to inspect the details.

A Controversy about Commandments

Matthew's story about the love commandment consists of a single question and a single answer. We will take up the question first and then the answer, searching the passage for the changes Matthew made in Mark's story and the reasons for the changes. In that way we will be able to assess Matthew's interpretation of Mark's interpretation of Jesus' interpretation of Deuteronomy 6:4-5 and Leviticus 19:18.

1. We begin with the hostile question Jesus was asked and the person who asked it. Two of Matthew's changes in Mark's text come at the beginning of the story of the love commandment. First, Matthew turns Mark's scribe, who is not said to belong to any party, into a lawyer, who belongs to the Pharisees. Second, Matthew turns a dialogue into a controversy by turning a serious question into a "question to test him" (Matthew 22:35). We need to look at both changes.

When we examined Mark's version of the story of the love commandment, we noticed that Mark uses the term "scribe" for the questioner, translating directly from Hebrew the name for a Jewish expert on Old Testament law. We noted that this term was accurate and comprehensible in Jewish circles but confusing in the larger non-Jewish world. Matthew apparently has seen the confusion the term "scribe" might well cause and has given us an alternative term, "lawyer." Matthew, who is generally said to have written the most Jewish of the Gospels, has here given us a less Jewish term for the expert who asks the question.

The second change makes a dialogue into a controversy. The question is asked "to test him." The older King James Version reads "tempting him"; the Greek term is the same one used in the story of what Satan did to Jesus in the wilderness for forty days after Jesus' baptism (Mark 1:13, Matthew 4:1). Clearly, Matthew wants us to see this as a hostile question, not a friendly one. By turning this dialogue into a controversy story he achieves a symmetry that Mark lacks—four controversy stories in a row. He shows Jesus in an atmosphere of unrelieved hostility during this last week of his ministry.

The question itself is innocent enough, "Which is the great commandment in the law?" (Matthew 22:36). It appears to be the equivalent of the question in Mark, "Which commandment is the first of all?" (Mark 12:28). It's an open-ended question. Where is the trick? What kind of trap does the question invite Jesus to walk into? There is very little clue in either the question or the answer. Only when we inspect the use to which Matthew shows Jesus putting the love commandment are we able to assess the answer I give here. The trap I see is this: Will Jesus deny to some part of the Old Testament the status of word of God by putting any commandment in a class by itself? If he says one commandment is "great," he can be accused of saying all the rest are junk. Not very subtle, is it? But then, trick questions usually aren't.

2. Matthew makes two significant changes in Jesus' answer to the question. The first change has to do with the quotation from Deuteronomy. According to Mark, we recall, Jesus quoted Deuteronomy 6:4-5 and Leviticus 19:18. According to Matthew, Jesus quoted only Deuteronomy 6:5 and Leviticus 19:18. The second change is the elimination of the questioner's reply and the alteration of the statement about what the love commandment covers. In Mark, the person who asks the question speaks twice and Jesus speaks twice. In Matthew each person speaks only once. In Mark the scribe says what Jesus means. In Matthew Jesus says what he means, and there is no further discussion. Furthermore, as we shall see, what Jesus says the love commandment is about in Matthew is not the same as what the scribe in Mark's story says the love commandment is about. We can take up each of these changes in the reply in turn.

What difference does it make whether Deuteronomy 6:4 is quoted or not? We looked at this question abstractly in chapter 2. There we observed that one effect of combining two commandments was to focus attention, by repeating "you shall," on *what is commanded*. There was a corresponding de-emphasis on the character of God, to which what was commanded was a response. Here we see in practice what we saw there abstractly. For the scribe in Mark's story, the love commandment was misnamed. He understood Jesus to have focused attention on God and called forth a response of appropriate worship. He hardly noticed the word "love." By contrast, in Matthew the love commandment is properly named. Jesus' sentences are imperatives, "You shall love . . . ." Jesus is the lawgiver, issuing commands on his own authority without reference to the character of God. Our attention is focused on what is commanded, "love," and on the commanding "you shall."

In both Mark and Matthew there is a statement about what the love commandment means. In Mark the scribe makes it; in Matthew Jesus says, "On these two commandments depend all the law and the prophets" (Matthew 22:40). We need to look at the meaning of "depend" and the way in which Jesus' answer confronts the trap set for him in the question.

In the century after Jesus, Jewish interpreters of the Old Testament worked out rules for interpretation. One of them used the Hebrew word corresponding to the Greek word here translated "depend." We don't know for sure that the Jewish rules of interpretation were as firmly fixed in Jesus' day as they were later. We don't know for sure how exact and technical the term "depend" was in Jesus' day. In general, however, we can see what is meant. If you didn't know a rule but did know the general principle, you could reason from the general principle to the rule. To describe the link you created by your reasoning, you would use the word "depend." Almost all the rules we set for small children are based on such general principles as "safety" or "health." If you know the principle of "safety," you can reason to the rule "Hold onto the railing." Then you could say the rule "Hold onto the railing" *depends* on the principle of "safety." Likewise, if you really understood the general principle of loving God and neighbor enunciated in Deuteronomy 6:5 and Leviticus 19:18, you would be able to reason to every law in the Old Testament. Rabbi Akiba would have agreed with this. He is the rabbi we met in chapter 2 who said that Leviticus 19:18 is "the greatest general principle in the Torah" (Sifra Leviticus 19:18). Can this be what Matthew understood Jesus to mean by "depend"? If so, there is nothing controversial about saying what everyone said, and it is nearly impossible to imagine why Matthew thought the question was hostile and the answer a piece of polemic.

Let's look at the explanation "On these two commandments depend all the law and the prophets" (Matthew 22:40) again. What if Jesus meant to say that rules exist only to explain general principles, which must be interpreted for specific situations? In that case, when toddlers go down stairs, the general principle "safety" might as reasonably suggest the rule "Always descend backwards with your hands on the step above you" as "Hold onto the railing." If you consider how hard it is for toddlers to reach railings, it may be a better rule. Or, to consider the case at hand, the general principle of the love commandment would function as a criterion to judge the adequacy or proper interpretation of any given rule. Rules, according to this kind of reasoning, have no status and no existence and no essential claim on us. Only the general principle exists and makes a moral claim. If Jesus, in Matthew, gave general principles this kind of status, he meant what the scribe in Mark's story took him to mean. To be sure, in Mark the scribe was thinking about worship, while in Matthew Jesus was thinking about the interpretation of scripture, but the love commandment has the same status and functions the same way in each case.

The statement which Jesus puts between his two quotations agrees with this second view of the role of a general principle. When Jesus says "This is the great and first commandment. And a second is like it," the two commandments are set apart from all others.

Putting the two commandments, Deuteronomy 6:5 and Leviticus 19:18, in a class by themselves was the thing that offended pious Jews. Pious Jews believed with all their hearts that each and every rule in the Old Testament was equally God's rule; to put these two in a class by themselves implied that some laws were God's laws more than others. Some one of their number used the question "Which is the great commandment in the law?" (Matthew 22:36) to dare Jesus to say that any one was in a category separate from the others. Jesus did not duck the question, evade the issue, or attempt to elude the trap. He replied directly to their question and the trick it contained. He quoted the two commandments and then underlined their significance, "On *these two* commandments depend *all* the law and the prophets" (Matthew 22:40, emphasis added). But then, having carefully set these two commandments apart from all others, he refused to declare the others junk. Rather, the two commandments are the key to the others, the criterion for interpreting all of Scripture.

We have completed our excursion through the verses which constitute Matthew's interpretation of the love commandment. Before we inspect the way Matthew sees Jesus using the love commandment, we must pause to make two observations about Matthew's understanding of Jesus in this story.

The first observation is that Jesus appears in Matthew's story as the Lord whom the church has known from Matthew's day to our own. Jesus sets the definitions, gives the explanations, renders the verdicts. In Mark, we meet a scribe who enters into conversation with Jesus as an equal. In Matthew, by way of contrast, Jesus' authority cannot be overlooked. You can oppose it, as the lawyer does, or you can acknowledge it as Christians do. But you can't fail to notice it. Which portrait is more likely to be true to Jesus' own ministry? It seems clear to me that Mark's portrait is the earlier. As stories about Jesus were told and retold among Christians, the tendency was to portray Jesus each time more as Lord. In Matthew's interpretation, Jesus holds the same ideas about the love commandment that he holds in Mark's interpretation. The difference isn't a matter of ideas but of the view of Jesus. At the same time the content of the ideas about the law, the confident boldness and sovereign freedom with which Jesus distinguishes what is "great" in Scripture, coaxes us away from the portrait of a wise teacher in Mark's interpretation and toward the portrait of the Lord of the church in Matthew's interpretation.

The second observation about Matthew's portrait of Jesus is that Jesus is a great interpreter of Scripture and teaches by his example how Christians ought to interpret the Old Testament. The scribe in Mark's story thought of one significant application of the love commandment. Jesus, in Matthew's interpretation, sets the love commandment as the key to the interpretation of Scripture which applies to many situations in all areas of life.

Unlocking Scripture

If we look at the Sermon on the Mount, Matthew 5—7, we can see how Matthew sees Jesus using the love commandment. The use of the love commandment in the Sermon on the Mount will occupy us for the rest of this chapter. It is true that the word "love" doesn't appear very often in the Sermon on the Mount (only in 5:43-48), but I propose that it controls the whole of the three chapters. Consider, for example, the Golden Rule, which stands at the end of the body of the Sermon on the Mount. This final statement should summarize the body of the sermon: "So whatever you wish that men would do to you, do so to them; for this is the law and the prophets" (Matthew 7:12).

The Golden Rule, which many of us learned by heart as children, sounds like a paraphrase of "You shall love your neighbor as yourself," doesn't it? Let's look at the ways the two verses are alike. The Golden Rule is not restricted but covers all humanity. When we looked at Leviticus 19:18 in chapter 2, we discovered that, while verses 17 and 18 cover citizens, verses 33 and 34 cover noncitizens. Within the two categories, citizens and noncitizens, everybody is included. So the Golden Rule covers precisely the same range of people as "You shall love your neighbor as yourself."

In the Golden Rule, Matthew 7:12, the criterion for appropriate action is the way you would like to be treated if you were in the other person's shoes. Isn't that just what we found the cryptic phrase "as yourself" to mean in Leviticus 19? There we picked out the sentence "The stranger...shall be...as the native...for you were strangers in the land of Egypt" (Leviticus 19:34) as the clue to the meaning of "as yourself." To know how to treat others, remember or imagine the situation they are in. Then you will know how they will want to be treated. Once again, the Golden Rule agrees with Leviticus 19:18.

The Golden Rule is like Leviticus 19:18 in another respect too, one which is unfortunate. Indeed, the Golden Rule is worse than Leviticus 19:18 in this respect. I mean that the Golden Rule can be taken as permission to be selfish, to make yourself the center of the moral universe and your own priorities the criterion of other people's behavior and even of public policy. Other people then become instruments in relation to you. This is true whether you are a person who intends to dominate your small world or one who just hopes to survive, neither making waves nor getting swamped by other people's waves. The Golden Rule teaches attention to other people to the limited extent required to achieve what you want. A proportionality is established and a calculation made in every human transaction.

Even granting that none of us knows exactly what love is, this doesn't sound at all like love, does it? Something has been lost when a paraphrase of the love commandment sounds like a selfishness commandment. What has happened that has turned the love commandment upside down? The answer is that Leviticus 19:18 has been paraphrased all by itself without reference to Deuteronomy 6:4-5 or even to Deuteronomy 6:5. That is, love of neighbor has been separated from love of God and both have been separated from their proper basis in the character of God. To keep the Golden Rule from degenerating into a selfishness commandment, it is very important never to think of it by itself but always to think of it as a clarification of part of the full commandment to love God and neighbor with full seriousness.

There is a quotation in Jewish literature which is quite a bit like Matthew 7:12.

> What you do not wish to happen to you, do not do to another. That is the whole Torah and all the rest is explanation; go and learn! (Shabbath 31a)

The person who stated this version of the Golden Rule was Rabbi Hillel, a slightly younger contemporary of Jesus. I do not think he stole this line from Jesus. Nor do I think Jesus copied Hillel. Rather, I think the existence of two rather similar sayings means that there was a rather extensive intellectual conversation in progress in Jesus' day on the subject of the love commandment. That is, these two versions of the Golden Rule, together with the quotations we looked at in chapter 2 and other materials, serve as evidence of Jesus' participation in and contribution to the intellectual life of his era.

Comparison of Hillel's version of the Golden Rule to the one in Matthew 7:12 yields one more similarity, a similarity which conceals a difference. Both versions say that they have to do with Scripture. But does Jesus mean the same thing in "This is the law and the prophets" as Rabbi Hillel means in "That is the whole Torah and all the rest is explanation"? Probably not. As we have seen, Jesus sets the love commandment apart from the remainder of the Old Testament law for the purpose of interpreting the law by the criterion of love. Matthew has selected this saying as a conclusion to the body of the sermon not only because it is a neatly crafted, snappy phrase, but also because it refers to both the love commandment and Scripture.

To see how Matthew sees Jesus interpreting the Bible in accordance with the love commandment, we will need to examine a portion of the earlier part of the body of the sermon. The first section of the body is Matthew 5:17-48. We looked at some of this material in chapter 1, without reference to the love commandment. Here we need to be especially attentive to the effect of the love commandment. Here is an outline:

5:17-20   Introduction
5:21-47   Six Examples
5:48   Conclusion

The introduction explains how the commandments in the Old Testament will be interpreted later in the chapter.

> Whoever then relaxes one of the least of these commandments and teaches men so, shall be called least in the kingdom of heaven; but he who does them and teaches them shall be called great in the kingdom of heaven. For I tell you, unless your righteousness exceeds that of the scribes and Pharisees, you will never enter the kingdom of heaven (Matthew 5:19-20).

Relaxing commandments is clearly the wrong way to interpret them. The opposite of relaxing must be the right way. When Jesus' contemporaries kept the law very thoroughly and carefully, they were called "righteous" or "perfect." The most enthusiastic keepers of the law, the most likely candidates for the term "righteous," were scribes, especially those of the party of Pharisees. So the right way to interpret the Old Testament, according to Matthew 5:17-20, is not by relaxing commandments but by outdoing the experts, by being super-righteous. Matthew 5:17-20 tells us what to look for as we inspect the rest of the chapter. We will ask, in each case: (1) What "relaxes"? (2) What constitutes super-righteousness? (3) Where does the love commandment come in?

In chapter 1 we looked at the first two of the six examples. Each is organized antithetically using a formula, "You have heard that it was said ... But I say to you." The first one, Matthew 5:21-26, was about murder. Jesus forbade not only murder but also anger and insults, the inward disposition which prompts murder and the actions which express the disposition in the absence of the forbidden act. The second one, Matthew 5:27-31, was about adultery. Jesus forbade not only adultery but also lust and skirt-chasing, the inward disposition and the action which expresses the disposition in the absence of the forbidden act. What "relaxes" these commandments? Limiting them to outward acts. What constitutes super-righteousness? Neither having the inward disposition which underlies what is forbidden nor acting out on a small scale what is forbidden. Where does the love commandment come in? The love commandment appears, I think, in the element of religious intensity. Jesus is saying, "You should obey the commandment 'You shall not kill' with all your heart and with all your soul and with all your mind and with all your strength." Such obedience will be a response which is adequate to the character of God, and it will, in fact, treat your neighbors as you would like to be treated if you were in their place. We might think of "relaxing" the command as halfheartedness and the super-righteousness required of Christians as wholeheartedness.

What Jesus recommends as a correct interpretation of Scripture and a recipe for super-righteousness reminds me of the scribe in Mark's story, the one we met in chapter 3. I argued there that Jesus approved of the scribe's single-minded focus on God alone. Here, too, we find Jesus approving of passionate intensity and single-minded concentration. In Mark's story the scribe's concentration resulted in ignoring distractions such as animal sacrifice, even when such distractions are in the Bible. Here, in the Sermon on the Mount, concentration on God alone does not involve ignoring or even relaxing *any* of the commandments.

The last of the six antitheses, Matthew 5:43-47, is the climax of the chapter. It is the only one of the six which uses the word "love." The fact that the word "love" appears in the last example in the series indicates that it is the goal of the whole chapter.

> You have heard that it was said, "You shall love your neighbor and hate your enemy." But I say to you, Love your enemies and pray for those who persecute you. . . . For if you love those who love you, what reward have you? (Matthew 5:43-44,46)

Nowhere in the Old Testament is there a verse which says "You shall love your neighbor and hate your enemy." The nearest is Leviticus 19:18, "You shall love your neighbor as yourself," which says nothing about enemies. What is quoted is both the commandment and the relaxing of the commandment. The phrase "hate your enemy" limits the commandment "love your neighbor" to those situations which lack hostility, those situations in which your neighbor is your friend. Reciprocity and mutuality among people, loving those who love you, is not what Leviticus 19:18 is about, according to the Sermon on the Mount.

We are ready for the three questions which we plan to ask of each example we take up. What "relaxes" Leviticus 19:18? Limiting it to mutuality and reciprocity, loving those who love you. What constitutes super-righteousness? Having the inward disposition to initiate love without trying to receive love in return. There is a definition of love in this passage which explains the source of the inward disposition. Loving your enemies is defined as praying for those who persecute you. Praying for people takes matters out of the realm of mutuality and reciprocity and puts matters in God's hand. When you have handed the hostility over to God, you no longer have it in your own hands. Your own attitude and behavior in relation to these hostile persons, these enemies, will no longer be characterized by hostility but by initiating love without trying to receive love in return. So where does the love commandment come in? The love commandment appears when matters are referred to God. According to this passage, social hostility and personal enmity are not purely human matters. If they were, mutuality and reciprocity, loving those who love you, would be an adequate rule to live by. Rather, the love commandment puts social relations in a larger context that the realm of practical politics. Combining Leviticus 19:18 with Deuteronomy 6:4-5 has made it impossible to limit loving your neighbor to loving those neighbors who are friends.

The final step on our tour of the first section of the Sermon on the Mount, a tour undertaken to observe how Matthew sees Jesus interpreting scripture, is the conclusion, "You, therefore, must be perfect, as your heavenly Father is perfect" (Matthew 5:48). The conclusion agrees with the introduction. What was called "righteousness [which] exceeds that of the scribes and Pharisees" in Matthew 5:20 (I named it "super-righteousness") is here called "perfection." In between were six significant examples of how the love commandment is the key to correct interpretation of the Bible and therefore to the correct way to live.

The conclusion, too, uses the love commandment. The lifestyle you work out after rigorous interpretation of Old Testament laws, interpretation according to the love commandment, will be a lifestyle which corresponds to God. It's quite a character-building program when the character that is built corresponds to the character of God! The same claim, that to love is to resemble God, is built into Deuteronomy 6:4-5. It is that claim which explains how the statements about God are related to the command to love God. When we looked at Deuteronomy 7:8-9 in chapter 2, we found that love was a constituent of God's own character, the wellspring and motivation for God's saving activity and commands.

Our excursion through the world of Matthew's interpretation of Jesus' interpretation of Deuteronomy 6:4-5 and Leviticus 19:18 is complete. In Mark we found a scribe who placed the love commandment in the context of Greek philosophy and thought it had to do with appropriate worship. Matthew, by contrast, portrays Jesus as placing it in the context of Jewish legal interpretation and applying it to the interpretation of Scripture. For the scribe in Mark's story, the intensity of his concentration on God made the words and commandments in the Old Testament of little importance. For Matthew, by contrast, the words and commandments in the Old Testament are very important. For Matthew, Jesus is to be distinguished from the later Jewish understanding not by how important he thinks the Old Testament is, but by how he uses the love commandment to make clear the radical character of what God demands.

5

Luke's Interpretation

Luke makes the story of the love commandment the introduction to a parable found only in his Gospel, the parable of the good Samaritan. Despite the obvious differences between Luke, on the one hand, and Matthew and Mark, on the other, the stories have numerous features in common.

Matthew 22:34-40	Mark 12:28-34	Luke 10:25-37
vs. 34-35	v. 28a	25 And behold, a lawyer stood up to put him to the test, saying,
v. 36	v. 28b	"Teacher, what shall I do to inherit eternal life?" 26 He said to him, "What is written in the law? How do you read?"
—	v. 29	—
vs. 37-39	vs. 30-31a	27 And he answered, "You shall love the Lord your God with all your heart, and with all your soul, and with all your strength, and with all your mind; and your neighbor as yourself."
v. 40	vs. 31b-34	28 And he said to him, "You have answered right; do this, and you will live." 29 But he, desiring to justify himself, said to

Jesus, "And who is my neighbor?"
30 Jesus replied, "A man was going down from Jerusalem to Jericho, and he fell among robbers, who stripped him and beat him, and departed, leaving him half dead.
31 Now by chance a priest was going down that road; and when he saw him he passed by on the other side.
32 So likewise a Levite, when he came to the place and saw him, passed by on the other side.
33 But a Samaritan, as he journeyed, came to where he was; and when he saw him, he had compassion, and went to him and bound up his wounds, pouring on oil and wine; then he set him on his own beast and brought him to an inn, and took care of him.
35 And the next day he took out two denarii and gave them to the innkeeper, saying, 'Take care of him; and whatever more you spend, I will repay you when I come back.'
36 Which of these three, do you think, proved neighbor to the man who fell among the robbers?"
37 He said, "The one who showed mercy on him." And Jesus said to him, "Go and do likewise."

Luke agrees with Matthew that the person who asks the question should be called a "lawyer" and that the question is asked to "test" Jesus. Luke also agrees with Matthew that the answer to the question is quoted from Deuteronomy 6:5 and Leviticus 19:18 and does not include Deuteronomy 6:4, a verse that was important in Mark's story.

The differences between Luke's story and those we found in Matthew and Mark are as striking as the similarities. The question is, of course, entirely different from the question in either Mark's story or Matthew's. In Luke's story, as in Mark's, the person who asks the question knows the answer in some way. Once the questioner in Mark's story heard the answer, Deuteronomy 6:4-5 and Leviticus 19:18, he understood immediately what it meant. In Luke's story, the questioner knows that the answer is Deuteronomy 6:5 and Leviticus 19:18 but has to ask what it means. In Mark the questioner explains the answer; in both Matthew and Luke, Jesus gives the explanation. But whereas in Matthew the explanation is very short, "On these two commandments depend all the law and the prophets" (Matthew 22:40), in Luke, Jesus' explanation is a fairly long parable, ending with a question which forces the questioner to answer his own question and thus help to create the explanation.

Most people who write about either the love commandment or the parable of the good Samaritan explain that there originally were two stories—one a parable, the other a controversy—and that some Christian of the generation before Luke's put them together because they share the word "neighbor," in verses 29 and 36. The evidence that the stories were originally separate is that verses 29 and 36 define "neighbor" from opposite sides.

We can observe the difference. In verse 29 the question "Who is my neighbor?" means "I am prepared to do a good deed. Who is an appropriate recipient?" Thus, "neighbor" is defined in verse 29 as "the recipient." Verse 36 is quite different. In verse 36 the question "Which of these three, do you think, proved neighbor to the man who fell among the robbers?" means "When I had need, who helped?" The answer is "the Samaritan." Thus, "neighbor" is defined in verse 36 as "the helper." Verse 29 is about giving help, with the neighbor as recipient; verse 36 is about receiving help, with the neighbor as the active agent who dispenses aid. It is, of course, quite possible to say that "neighbor" means both the giver of assistance and the recipient of assistance and that neighborliness is a matter of both giving and receiving. Both verses 29 and 36 define neighbor correctly; the difference is that they look at "neighbor" from different sides. The argument that the story of the love commandment was originally separate from the parable of the good Samaritan is based on the fact that verses 29 and 36 look at "neighbor" differently.

Arguments about how the two stories were originally separate do not take us very far toward understanding either story (if they ever were separate) or the story as a whole (whether composite or original). I have rehearsed the argument primarily because the observation that "neighbor" is seen from different sides is an important one. I take that observation, not as evidence of the composite nature of Luke 10:25-37, but as a clue to the meaning Jesus attaches, in this story, to Leviticus 19:18 and as a clue to Jesus' answer to the lawyer's question.

Our tour of the world of the love commandment gets more and more complicated as we go along. We began with two quotations from the Old Testament and added Jesus' interpretation. Then we began to track down the various New Testament interpretations of Jesus' interpretation. Mark's story seemed the closest to Jesus' own life and ministry. In the last chapter we compared Matthew to Mark and saw how Matthew interpreted both Jesus and Mark's interpretation of Jesus. Here we have to compare Luke's story to Matthew's as well as to Mark's and to the interpretive achievemennt of Jesus himself. There is no end in sight of the complexities involved in interpreting multiple interpretations of Jesus' interpretation. Remember the parent in the story with which this book began, the one who saw no end in sight and told the child, "It's elephants all the way down." That parent may have grasped our situation in trying to understand the love commandment.

Mapping Luke's Gospel

Let's begin with the setting of the story. The setting of both Mark's and Matthew's stories was the last week of Jesus' ministry, while he was in the public area of the temple in Jerusalem. How about Luke's story? Is it located there also? No, Luke's story is found in a section which takes place on the way to Jerusalem. The section begins, "When the days drew near for him to be received up, he set his face to go to Jerusalem" (Luke 9:51). The next section begins, "when he had said this, he went on ahead, going up to Jerusalem" (Luke 19:28).

Between these two verses Jesus has a traveling ministry with very few indications of the direction of travel. It might be better to think of it as a wandering ministry with a beginning place and an ending place. The section begins with a story about rejection by a "village of the Samaritans" (Luke 9:51-57) and has near its end two stories located in Jericho: the healing of a blind man (Luke 18:35-43) and the story of Zacchaeus (Luke 19:1-10). The implication is that Jesus is traveling from his home in Galilee southward through Samaria to Jerusalem. The story of the love commandment is located early in this section. What does Luke do when Jesus gets to Jerusalem and teaches in the temple?

1. Mark 11:27—12:13/ Matthew 21:23-46/ Luke 20:1-19. Controversy over Jesus' authority, including the story of the vineyard (Matthew adds a second parable).

2. Mark 12:13-17/ Matthew 22:15-22/ Luke 20:20-26. Controversy over paying taxes to Caesar.

3. Mark 12:18-27/ Matthew 22:23-33/ Luke 20:27-40. Controversy over the resurrection.

4. Mark 12:28-34/ Matthew 22:34-40/ -----. Discussion about the law (Matthew turns it into a controversy; Luke omits it).

Luke has followed Mark's outline at least as well as Matthew did. He copies Mark almost exactly in the three controversy stories. Apparently Luke has the same problem that Matthew had with the asymmetry of Mark's arrangement—three controversies and a discussion. Matthew solved the problem of asymmetry by turning the story of the love commandment into a fourth controversy; Luke solves the problem by dropping it out. Either way, the arrangement is tidier. For Luke there is the additional advantage that he is free to put the story of the love commandment earlier in his Gospel, where the parable of the good Samaritan is near his other story about Samaritans (9:51-57).

Inheriting Eternal Life—Luke 10:25

The story Luke knows about the love commandment begins like Matthew's. The person who asks the question is a "lawyer" and the question is asked "to test him."

The question itself is, however, as different from Matthew's as it is from Mark's, "Teacher, what shall I do to inherit eternal life?" The question is the same as that asked by the rich man in another story:

> And a ruler asked him, "Good Teacher, what shall I do to inherit eternal life?" And Jesus said to him, "Why do you call me good? No one is good but God alone. You know the commandments: 'Do not commit adultery, Do not kill, Do not steal, Do not bear false witness, Honor your father and mother.'" And he said, "All these I have observed from my youth." And when Jesus heard it, he said to him, "One thing you still lack. Sell all that you have and distribute to the poor, and you will have treasure in heaven; and come, follow me." But when he heard this he became sad, for he was very rich (Luke 18:18-23).

The same story in much the same words may be found in Matthew 19:16-22 and Mark 10:17-22, but I have quoted from Luke because in this chapter we are interested in what Luke says.

What can we learn from comparing the story of the rich man to Luke's story about the love commandment? It is clear, in the first place, that the question is an ultimate question, having to do with salvation. To inherit eternal life is to be saved. The answer in each case is to refer the questioner to what he already knows by quoting Old Testament law. Here Jesus quotes bits of the Ten Commandments; in chapter 10 he gets the questioner to quote Deuteronomy 6:5 and Leviticus 19:18. When the questioner follows up Jesus' reply with an indication that he wants to know more, Jesus in each case explains his answer. The words "Come, follow me" in Luke 8:22 are a call to discipleship, the same formula Jesus used when he called Simon and Andrew.

> And Jesus said to them, "Follow me, and I will make you become fishers of men." And immediately they left their nets and followed him (Mark 1:17-18).

The discipleship to which Jesus called Simon and Andrew required them to devote themselves so single-mindedly to following Jesus that they left behind the commercial fishing business which was their everyday reality. In the same way, Jesus calls the rich man to devotion so single-minded that he will leave his possessions behind. Jesus does not criticize the rich man or his piety; he offers him a lesson in single-minded discipleship.

The story of the rich man has themes that remind me of Mark's interpretation of the love commandment. The rich man lacks the religious intensity of the scribe in Mark's story. He knows the laws in the Old Testament and keeps them faithfully. But he doesn't hear the voice of God; he doesn't focus his attention on God alone. There are also themes reminiscent of Matthew's interpretation. The rich man would not be so confident that he obeys the laws fully and completely if he knew that Jesus interpreted the law in Matthew 5 as requiring not only outward obedience but also inward obedience, which I characterized as obedience "with all your heart and with all your soul and with all your mind and with all your strength." It seems to me that when Jesus calls this particular person to discipleship, he calls him to obedience to the love commandment.

The story of the rich man also has themes that remind me of Luke's interpretation of the love commandment. The first, of course, is obvious: The same question is asked. The other is almost as obvious: There is a concern for the poor and the victim in both passages. The story of the good Samaritan deals with the immediate needs of, and practical assistance for, the victim of a mugging. The story of the rich man recommends not only the religious intensity of single-minded following but also a practical and prudent divestiture and redistribution of wealth. I wasn't sure the scribe in Mark had any real sense of what loving a neighbor might mean. He seemed to respond almost entirely to love of God. Matthew's interpretation also seemed to me to focus on Deuteronomy 6:5, although the full implications of obeying the Old Testament laws took the neighbor more seriously. But Luke's interpretation focuses directly on Leviticus 19:18.

The observation that the question "What shall I do to inherit eternal life?" belongs not only to Luke's story of the love commandment but also to Luke's story of the rich man has led us far afield. We need to return now to Luke's direct interpretation of the love commandment.

Luke 10:26-29

Jesus doesn't answer the question directly but instead calls on the lawyer to quote the Old Testament. The lawyer quotes the two passages we know as the love commandment, Deuteronomy 6:5 and Leviticus 19:18, splicing them together to make a single sentence. Jesus, as we might expect, approves his answer. We know this is a controversy story because the narrator tells us at the beginning that the lawyer asked the question "to test him." However, no trap has yet appeared. If there was a trap in the question, Jesus hasn't walked into it. Rather, he lets the lawyer, who wants to trap him, indicate the direction he wants the conversation to go.

It is not until the lawyer speaks for the third time that the trap appears. The lawyer asks a question which makes it clear what he wants Jesus to talk about. "Who is my neighbor?" (Luke 10:29). The narrator takes us inside the lawyer's head, revealing his intentions to us with the words "desiring to justify himself." Here is where we should look for the trap. The lawyer intends to prove that his own practice is correct and that Jesus' practice is wrong.

The trap concerns the definition of "neighbor" or the kinds of people it is appropriate to associate with. Jews did not socialize with Gentiles, and pious Jews kept their distance from less pious Jews. Jesus was known to associate with riffraff of all kinds. If he could be trapped into a definition of neighbor as shockingly broad as his practice, he could be accused of breaking the law. We can see how seriously Jews took definitions of proper associates by looking at Acts 10 and 11. The story explains how Peter, a Jewish Christian and one of Jesus' closest associates, happened to preach to Gentiles. Here are two excerpts from the story:

> He fell into a trance and saw the heaven opened, and something descending, like a great sheet, let down by four corners upon the earth. In it were all kinds of

animals and reptiles and birds of the air. And there came a voice to him, "Rise, Peter; kill and eat." But Peter said, "No, Lord; for I have never eaten anything that is common or unclean." And the voice came to him again a second time, "What God has cleansed, you must not call common." This happened three times, and the thing was taken up at once to heaven (Acts 10:10-16).

Shortly after this incident, messengers come from Cornelius, a Roman centurion who was attracted to Judaism, requesting that Peter speak to the friends, relatives, servants, and other dependents assembled at Cornelius' house. This is what Peter said to them:

"You yourselves know how unlawful it is for a Jew to associate with or to visit any one of another nation; but God has shown me that I should not call any man common or unclean. So when I was sent for, I came without objection" (Acts 10:28-29).

The story goes on to show how this large Gentile household became Christian. But we have seen enough to observe that Peter needed a message from God to persuade him to preach to Gentiles. If a close associate of Jesus required that kind of persuasion to broaden his definition of neighbor, what will it take to persuade the hostile questioner in our story? These, at any rate, are the odds Jesus faces when he answers the question "Who is my neighbor?" with the story of the good Samaritan.

There is something to be said for the strategy of answering a hostile question with a story. Consider how easy it would have been for the lawyer to reject Jesus' interpretation of "You shall love your neighbor as yourself" if Jesus had said "I say to you, Love your enemies" (Matthew 5:44). Even though a story may include the same people in the circle of appropriate associates, Jesus is wise to tell the story. The questioner, no matter how hostile, will have to listen all the way through and may be forced to see something he hasn't seen before.

Luke 10:30-35

The story of the good Samaritan is a familiar one. It is read often and for many purposes. Because we are reading this parable as part of our tour through the world of the love commandment, it is important to ask where the love commandment comes in. Clearly the parable has to do with Leviticus 19:18, "You shall love your neighbor as yourself." The question is: What does it seize on as the key to interpreting Leviticus 19:18? Many people will answer that the parable of the good Samartian seizes the word "neighbor" as the key because that is what the questioner asked about. Others will answer that it seizes the word "love" as the key because only that word expresses the extraordinary deeds of the Samaritan. But I suggest that the parable seizes the phrase "as yourself" as the key to Leviticus 19:18 because only that phrase explains the difference in the meaning of "neighbor" in verses 29 and 36, and because only that phrase relates the parable to the original question in verse 25 about inheriting eternal life.

The best way to hear a parable is the way the first audience heard it, from beginning to end. The titles we know for parables often don't help us hear them that way. Here is an example. What would you call a story that began

"There was a man who had two sons" (Luke 15:11)? You might think of titles such as "Father and Sons" or "The Two Sons." The title we usually use for the story, "The Prodigal Son," doesn't help us begin at the beginning, does it? Here is another example. What would you call a story that began "The kingdom of heaven is like a householder who went out early in the morning to hire laborers for his vineyard" (Matthew 20:1)? You might think of titles such as "The Vineyard Owner" or "Hiring." The title we usually use, "The Laborers in the Vineyard," comes from the first sentence, to be sure, but it distracts our attention away from the owners toward the laborers and makes it hard to read the parable from beginning to end. The parable of the good Samaritan is another example of the title which makes it hard to read the parable from beginning to end. What should we call a story that begins "A man was going down from Jerusalem to Jericho, and he fell among robbers" (Luke 10:30)? Judging from the first sentence we might title it "The Mugging" or "Disaster on the Jericho Road." My only point is that we won't understand the parable unless we begin at the beginning, in this case with the victim of a mugging.

The victim could be anybody, even you or I. The English is vague: "A man." The Greek is even more indefinite, if that is possible: "Some human being." The first words invite us to recall the place and, even if we know it only by reputation, to experience the terror, pain, and degradation of the event which takes place there. It is all over in a minute, and we are left in some ditch to think about what has happened and to wonder if we are to die in this God-forsaken place. The mental part may be the worst.

Somebody comes by, two people in fact, representatives of organized religion. These people know all about loving their neighbors. Organized religion is a good thing, and its representatives are some of the world's finest people. Incredulous, we watch them from our place in the ditch as they pass us by. What shall we think now about organized religion? We are in no mood to make excuses, that's certain. Waiting to be rescued turns out to be a lonely and agonizing business. We begin to consider alternative fates. What if the outlaws return to finish us off?

Somebody else comes along, somebody worse than an outlaw. Outlaws, after all, might have hearts of gold, but Samaritans are beneath contempt. Insults and avenging insults. That's all they think of. And that's all the dealings we ever have with them. That's the way it always has been as far back as we can recall. It requires no law to prohibit us from fraternizing with such scum. Why, oh why, is a slimy character like this stopping? There is nothing more to steal, is there? We're grateful for the rescue, of course. Or are we? Does he intend murder? Rape? No, he's administering first aid, organizing transportation. Perhaps he plans to sell us as slaves or kidnap us for ransom. Is this a rescue or isn't it? It has some of the qualities of a nightmare. Putting us up in an inn is just too much. There is no such thing as a compassionate Samaritan. Everyone knows that. But here is a Samaritan overflowing with compassion, heaping one good deed upon another. Our gratitude for his compassion is mixed with our amazement at who it is that has helped us and a vague resentment that we have an enemy to thank for our rescue from a desperate situation.

Luke 10:36-37

The story ends. To my way of thinking, the clue that the story is meant to be read from the victim's point of view is that Jesus asks the concluding question from the victim's point of view. Let me rearrange the words to bring out the meaning. "*To the man who fell among robbers,* which of these three proved neighbor?" The hostile questioner who initiated this entire conversation has heard the story from the victim's point of view. He knows what "neighbor" means. The neighbor is "the one who showed mercy" (Luke 10:37). His shock at having an enemy as a helper shows through in his refusal to identify the helper as a Samaritan.

Jesus' reply "Go and do likewise" (Luke 10:37) is as challenging as it is unspecific. What is it that Jesus wants done? What is to be imitated? What you think Jesus wants done depends to a large extent on where you think the love commandment comes in. Let's inspect the options.

If you think the word "neighbor" in "You shall love your neighbor as yourself" is the key to Luke 10:25-37, you will say "Go and do likewise" means "Hunt for a victim and do something to help." The good Samaritan will be your model. You will have to ignore the fact that Samaritans are enemies. And you will not be able to make sense of the shift in the point of view from which neighbor is defined in the passage.

If you think the word "love" is the key, you will say "Go and do likewise" is a call to ever deeper compassion, suitably expressed. You will set the action in response to a need in the forefront of your consciousness and steadfastly ignore the identity of the victim. You will be especially attentive to the piling up of details in verses 34 and 35 of all the things the Samaritan did. But you will not be able to make sense of the point of view from which "neighbor" is defined in verse 36.

I have already proposed that "as yourself" in "You shall love your neighbor as yourself" is the key to Luke 10:25-37. Let's explore this proposal. The story invites us to remember or imagine what it is like to be a victim and then to think about and see the world from the victim's point of view. The proverbial phrase about walking a mile in someone else's moccasins captures something of the point. So does the idea of treating people as you would like to be treated if you were in their place. If we found the Golden Rule (Matthew 7:12) at the end of this story it would mean "Whatever you wish that someone would do to you if you were a victim, do so to them when they are victims." The story from the victim's point of view would keep the Golden Rule from being the calculation of advantage that I worried about when we looked at the Golden Rule in chapter 4. When Jesus says "Go and do likewise," what does he want done? According to the interpretation I have proposed, he means something like "Go, experience life as a victim and you will know how to love your neighbor as yourself."

Has the first question the lawyer asked, "What shall I do to inherit eternal life?" been answered? The lawyer didn't care about an answer to the question. But Jesus might well have answered it anyway. I think the parable of the good Samaritan answers the question "What shall I do to inherit eternal life?" as well as the question "Who is my neighbor?". The answer to the question of course is that nothing you *do* will put you in line for the mercy of God. You are as helpless to secure salvation as a victim in a ditch. The question misses the point. Furthermore, as long as the question is raised that way ("What shall I do?"), salvation will be a total surprise, quite unwelcome and a great shock. You will be as unprepared for God's grace as a victim is to receive help from a mortal enemy. The shock of salvation will have all the religious intensity of the scribe in Mark's story of the love commandment, who knew in his bones that God alone is God "and there is no other but he; and to love him with all the heart, and with all the understanding, and with all the strength, and to love one's neighbor as oneself, is much more than. . ." (Mark 12:32-33) all pious acts and anything you can do.

I invite you to think of the story of the good Samaritan as an interpretation of Leviticus 19:34:

> The stranger who sojourns with you shall be to you as the native among you, and you shall love him as yourself; for you were strangers in the land of Egypt: I am the LORD your God.

Being "strangers in the land of Egypt" functions in two ways. The experience of slavery in Egypt and the experience of victimization on the road to Jericho are clues to how your neighbor is to be loved. At the same time, the experience of exodus out of slavery in Egypt and the experience of being rescued after a mugging by an unlikely and not altogether welcome agent are the basis for loving your neighbor. It is an event of salvation which mandates a corresponding love.

The love commandment works in two ways in this passage in Luke. First, it makes the victim's point of view normative for social action and the moral life. Second, it makes the humbling experience of receiving salvation the basis for whatever actions we take.

6

John's Interpretation

The Gospel of John is different from the first three gospels in a number of ways, and the differences affect the way the love commandment is handled. We need to look, first, at some characteristics of the Gospel and then at its treatment of the love commandment.

The Gospel of John is not so different from Matthew, Mark and Luke that you would mistake it for something other than a Gospel. Clearly, it is a Gospel. It ends with a trial, crucifixion, and resurrection, just like the others. Before that last sequence is a ministry composed of teaching and marvelous deeds, just like the others. The author of John seems to have known Mark's Gospel, as the authors of Matthew and Luke did. But, unlike the authors of Matthew and Luke, the author of John doesn't copy out passages from Mark. He uses some stories in the same order as Mark but he rewrites them completely.

Three characteristics of the Gospel of John differentiate it from the other Gospels to a degree and in a way that will help us with the love commandment. The first characteristic is *writing style and plot construction*. In the first three Gospels, Jesus makes statements that may be said to be short and snappy; in the Gospel of John he makes speeches that run for most of a chapter. The style of John is meditational. A topic is introduced and considered not from one angle but from several. Key words, such as "see," are introduced and then used to mean several different things. In the first three Gospels Jesus rushes from one scene to another; the Gospel of John has fewer scenes and less action. The word "tableau" comes to mind when I think of the way John constructs scenes.

The second characteristic is the *way Jesus is portrayed*. There is no birth narrative like the ones in Matthew and Luke. Instead, the Gospel of John begins at the beginning of Jesus' ministry, like the Gospel of Mark. The prologue to the Gospel of John tells us how we are to regard Jesus.

> In the beginning was the Word. . . .All things were made through him. . . .The Word was God. . . .The Word became flesh. . . .No one has ever seen God; the only Son. . .has made him known (John 1:1,3,14,18).

Jesus is the creative Word God spoke at the beginning of the world, when "God said, 'Let there be light'; and there was light" (Genesis 1:3). That creative Word, which is identical with God's own being, became flesh, with the result that we can know God, something not otherwise possible. Did I paraphrase adequately the phrases I quoted? If I did, we can now see some special characteristics of Jesus, as portrayed in the Gospel of John.

1. Jesus is, from the very beginning, Lord. All the earliest Christians, like Christians today, confessed Jesus as Lord. The sermon Peter preached on the day of Pentecost, surely a typical formulation, ends emphatically, "Let all the house of Israel therefore know assuredly that God has made him both Lord and Christ, this Jesus whom you crucified" (Acts 2:36). The sermon in Acts differs considerably from the Gospel of John. In Acts Jesus becomes Lord after the resurrection and ascension; in John he was Lord before creation. The authors of Matthew, Mark, and Luke know that Jesus is Lord, but they don't make their confession the subject matter for their Gospels; the author of the Gospel of John makes the Lord he confesses as much the subject matter as the stories he knows about Jesus.

The Greek word translated "Word" is *logos,* which means two things. First, as I have already indicated, it refers us to Genesis 1 where God creates by speaking. Second, it is a term in Greek philosophy referring to the first principles of the universe: whatever constitutes the universe, holds it together, and makes it run. The scribe in Mark's story of the love commandment thought Jesus said that Deuteronomy 6:4-5 and Leviticus 19:18 told him how to get his life tuned to the rhythms of the universe. The love commandment was a moral first principle, to his way of thinking. If he ever became a Christian, I think he would have like the way the Gospel of John pictures Jesus: as Lord from before the beginning of the world, and as Logos, the first principle of all creation.

2. In the second place, however, Jesus is a genuinely historical person. The Gospel of John would never agree with anyone who said Jesus only *seemed* to live a human life. Indeed, the word "flesh" is chosen in preference to the word "body" to make sure no one could ever say that the Word of God borrowed a body for a while and then left it when it wasn't convenient to use it any longer. Jesus, according to the Gospel of John, was no spook. The Gospel of John insists that Jesus was fully human.

3. In the third place, Jesus is transparent, in the Gospel of John, to what God is doing. By using the word "transparent" I mean that when you look at Jesus you see through him to God. Jesus' actions are actions which reveal God; his words are words which make God known.

Our tour of the world of the love commandment has taken a detour through the characteristics of the Gospel of John, characteristics which are pertinent to John's interpretation of the love commandment. We have looked at two such characteristics so far, writing style and the portrayal of Jesus. One more remains, *the treatment of time and history.*

The Gospel of John has a distinctive view of time. We live most of our lives by what we may call "linear time," time which runs along a line from before to after, from past to future, from early to late. We measure our time with clocks and calendars into minutes and hours, decades and millennia. Sometimes we say that Jesus lived in the past, he died in the past and rose from the dead in the past, and he will come again in the future. Some people expect a last judgment at the end of the world; others expect it after they die. The Gospel of John, however, makes future events into present realities. A good example is a dialogue in the chapter on the raising of Lazarus:

> Jesus said to her, "Your brother will rise again." Martha said to him, "I know that he will rise again in the resurrection at the last day." Jesus said to her, "I am the resurrection and the life; he who believes in me, though he die, yet shall he live, and whoever lives and believes in me shall never die. Do you believe this?" She said to him, "Yes, Lord; I believe that you are the Christ, the Son of God, he who is coming into the world" (John 11:23-27).

Martha believes in a resurrection sometime in the distant future, at the end of the world. Jesus' reply takes the resurrection she believes in out of the future and puts it in the present. Not only that. Jesus says that he himself, Jesus, whose own death is still in the future, is already the resurrection. By any ordinary reckoning of time and by the usual Christian confession, this is impossible. Jesus has to die before he can be raised. It stands to reason: first the crucifixion, then the resurrection. Notice what the author of the Gospel of John has done here. First, he has made Jesus embody the word "resurrection." "I am the resurrection" is another way of saying "The word resurrection became flesh and dwelt among us." Jesus, as he is portrayed here, is transparent to God's purpose, which shows through what Jesus says. Second, he has caused to stand before Martha what she knows to be the ultimate and eventual purpose of God. He has made the future salvation a present reality. The salvation that belongs to "the last day" occurs right now.

Another example of the way the future becomes a present reality in the Gospel of John may help. This one concerns the Last Judgment. By Last Judgment I refer to a big court scene, encompassing heaven and earth, in which all of human history is reviewed and all injustices corrected and compensated for. You can read some of these scenarios in the New Testament, most notably in the Book of Revelation. The richest imagery and most fully developed scenes are to be found, however, in later Christian art and literature. For example, have you ever read Jonathan Edwards' sermon "Sinners in the Hands of an Angry God" (1741)? The author of the Gospel of John has a distinctly different view of the Last Judgment.

> For God sent the Son into the world, not to condemn the world, but that the world might be saved through him. He who believes in him is not condemned; he who does not believe is condemned already (John 3:17-18).

In the Gospel of John, Jesus makes it clear that the purpose of judgment is not condemnation. Rather, God intends salvation. Furthermore, the judgment isn't far off in the future but right now. Finally, the criterion for judgment is not just and righteous behavior but rather belief in Jesus. The phrases about believing in Jesus also occur in the dialogue about the resurrection which was our first example. In each case they refer to current, personal, active belief, not to some past confession, long neglected but somehow magically efficacious. The author of the Gospel of John wants to make it clear that salvation is offered in every minute of time to anyone who believes in Jesus. Did you notice that the dialogue concludes with a question and answer that sound like a confession of faith someone gives when joining the church in our own day?

Question: "Do you believe this?"
Answer: "Yes Lord; I believe that you are the Christ, the Son of God."
Believing in Jesus implies, in the Gospel of John, joining the community of believers, the community of salvation.

The overview just completed of some general characteristics of the Gospel of John constitutes the first phase of our excursion into the world of the love commandment as it is interpreted in the Gospel of John. It is in this terrain that the love commandment will be found and in this context that it will be interpreted.

Mapping John's Gospel

Our first discovery, when we go in search of the love commandment, is that nowhere in the Gospel of John is either Deuteronomy 6:5 or Leviticus 19:18 quoted. Does this mean that the Gospel of John knows nothing of love? Not at all. Our second discovery comes when we look in a concordance to see where the term "love" is to be found in the Gospel of John. The list of verses is enormous! There are more entries for John than for Matthew, Mark and Luke added together. We also note that the verses where the word "love" is used are concentrated near the end of the Gospel of John, in chapters 13 through 17. What shall we make of these odd discoveries? The answer, in general, is that the author of the Gospel of John has written a meditation on what others quote. If we survey chapters 13 through 17 we should be able to see how the love commandment is interpreted in the Gospel of John. In addition, we should be able to pick out some key verses which represent with special clarity elements of that interpretation.

Chapter 13 begins with the last supper Jesus had with his disciples before he was arrested. Matthew, Mark, and Luke all tell the same basic story about this supper, including the familiar words about the loaf and the cup, "This is my body...This is my blood..." (Mark 14:22,24). No after-dinner speeches are reported. By contrast, the Gospel of John does not repeat the words of institution but rather describes a lengthy after-dinner speech. Somewhere in the middle of the meal, the author says "during supper" (John 13:2), Jesus washed the feet of his disciples, playing the role of a servant. He also told them what it all meant:

> If I then, your Lord and Teacher, have washed your feet, you also ought to wash one another's feet. For I have given you an example, that you also should do as I have done to you (John 13:14-15).

I think the author wants to tell us something about the meaning of the Lord's Supper. Jesus doesn't say, "This is my body"; rather, he offers a service, using parts of his body. He doesn't say, "Do this in remembrance of me" (Luke 22:19), but the principle of imitating his activity is the same. The setting, then, of chapters 13 through 17 is the Last Supper, beginning in the middle of the meal. The next section of the Gospel of John begins in 18:1 with the words "When Jesus had spoken these words, he went forth. . . ." Between these we have an after-dinner speech which continues through chapter 16 and ends with a prayer in chapter 17.

An After-Dinner Speech

The speeches are Jesus' last will and testament. Wills, in antiquity and in the present, bequeath a legacy. Ancient legacies usually consisted of real estate or personal property, as do modern ones. In addition, sages and wise men wrote literary testaments, passing on their best thoughts to their spiritual heirs. Those who read such books were admonished concerning moral behavior and an appropriate lifestyle, exemplified by the life of the person writing the will. In chapter 2, for example, we looked at two small quotations from a Jewish work in the form of a testament. In them we found admonitions such as "Keep, therefore, my children, the law of God" (T. Issachar 5:1), based on the life of the writer, "I loved the Lord" (T. Issachar 7:6).

In the speech he makes in the Gospel of John, Jesus leaves a legacy. Some sentences use words such as "leave," "give," and "send."

> But the Counselor, the Holy Spirit, whom the Father will send in my name, he will teach you all things, and bring to your remembrance all that I have said to you. Peace I leave with you; my peace I give to you (John 14:26-27).

It is easy to see that the direct legacy, in this passage, is "peace." It may not be quite as easy to see that the teachings of Jesus are also bequeathed in this passage. The Holy Spirit is a substitute teacher, sent in Jesus' name to teach new lessons and call to mind those lessons already learned.

Other sentences give a legacy in the form of a promise. "I will come again and will take you to myself, that where I am you may be also" (John 14:3). Still other sentences give a legacy in the form of a prayer:

> I do not pray for these only, but also for those who believe in me through their word, that they may all be one. . . . I made known to them thy name, and I will make it known, that the love with which thou hast loved me may be in them, and I in them (John 17:20-21, 26).

These words are a prayer not only because the word "pray" is used but also because they address God directly. A prayer which blesses the heirs is a regular feature of ancient last wills and testaments. The blessing requested will not be denied by God but becomes part of the legacy of the person, in this case Jesus, whose will this is. What is it that Jesus bequeaths in this passage and to whom is it bequeathed? In this passage, Jesus bequeaths the unity of the church with the words "that they may all be one," and he bequeaths it to all future generations of Christians, including our own.

This passage is an important one to many modern Christians. A church divided into competing denominations and confessional groups is a scandal, say these Christians, an offense against Christ, a repudiation of his blessing. Organizational efforts toward reconciliation, cooperation in specific tasks, and eventual church union are the result of passionate engagement with this passage. Such efforts are called "ecumenical" or "interdenominational" and range from local efforts to national and worldwide organizations such as Church Women United and the World Council of Churches. Nineteenth-century founders of the movement of Christians which uses the name "Disciples of Christ" were enthusiasts of Christian unity, and many of their twentieth-century heirs share their enthusiasm for this gift of Christ. The unity which is Christ's gift to the church is described in this passage by the words "that the love with which thou hast loved me may be in them, and I in them" (John 17:26). If we wanted to put this in different words, we could say that Christian unity is participation in God's love.

Much of chapters 13 through 17 is about participation in God's love. I found no less than seven passages which touch on this theme.

1. "A new commandment I give to you, that you love one another; even as I have loved you, that you also love one another. By this all men will know that you are my disciples, if you have love for one another" (John 13:34-35).

2. "If you love me, you will keep my commandments" (John 14:15).

3. "He who has my commandments and keeps them, he it is who loves me; and he who loves me will be loved by my Father, and I will love him and manifest myself to him" (John 14:21).

4. "If a man loves me, he will keep my word, and my Father will love him, and we will come to him and make our home with him. He who does not love me does not keep my words" (John 14:23-24).

5. "As the Father has loved me, so have I loved you; abide in my love. If you keep my commandments, you will abide in my love, just as I have kept my Father's commandments and abide in his love" (John 15:9-10).

6. "This is my commandment, that you love one another as I have loved you" (John 15:12).

7. "This I command you, to love one another" (John 15:17).

There are several ways in which the *participatory character* of love is indicated in these passages. The first is the use of the word "abide" in passage 5, John 15:9-10. Love, in this passage, is an environment, something you can live in. The second is what we might call the principle of imitation. We can see it in several of the passages: for example, "even as I have loved you, that you also love one another" in passage 1 (John 13:34), or "that you love one another as I have loved you" in passage 6 (John 15:12). We recall that Jesus' after-dinner speech follows his washing the disciples' feet, an activity he explained by saying, "I have given you an example, that you also should do as I have done to you" (John 13:15). You can find other examples. The third way in which the participatory character of love is indicated is the phrase "one another." The love which is commanded in passages 1, 6, and 7 (John 13:34-35; 15:12; 15:17) is mutual and reciprocal. Reciprocal love for other Christians creates an environment in which church members abide and in which Christ is present. To maintain such an environment of mutual love is to maintain an environment which not only Jesus but also his Father will call home. The Gospel of John says all these things and much more about Christian participation in God's love.

We said at the beginning that these addresses are an interpretation of the love commandment. Now we are ready to inspect the interpretations of Leviticus 19:18 and Deuteronomy 6:4-5 separately and then observe the way the two quotations work together.

Leviticus 19:18 is not quoted directly but appears repeatedly in the form "love one another." The author of John chooses this form intentionally. The focus here is not on "the neighbor" but on fellow Christians. It is not on giving without expectation of return as in the commandment "Love your enemies" (Matthew 5:44) which we examined in chapter 4 but on reciprocal and mutual love given in reasonable expectation of return. What has happened to Christian concern for the outsider, the foreigner, the sojourner? Does the Gospel of John simply not care about outsiders? Not really. The idea in the Gospel of John is that the love Christians have for each other will be so noticeable and attractive that outsiders will want to become insiders and thus to participate in mutual love. Jesus prays "that they may become perfectly one, so that the world may know that thou hast sent me and hast loved them even as thou hast loved me" (John 17:23). Here the unity of Christians, based on their love for each other, is a sermon for the instruction of the world outside the church. The inner life of the church is itself an instrument of Christian mission.

Deuteronomy 6:4-5 is not quoted either. In fact, nowhere in the Gospel of John will you find anything about loving God. True, you find sentences that begin "God loves . . ." but none say that someone loves God. It looks as though the author of the Gospel of John thinks you shouldn't use the same words about God that you use about people. Maybe he would think that "worship" is given to God and "love" is given to people. Near the end of the New Testament there is a letter which explains the way the Gospel of John uses Deuteronomy 6:4-5. "In this is love, not that we loved God but that he loved us" (1 John 4:10). What the Gospel of John has done, according to this early interpretation, is to make the commandment to love God with all your heart, soul, mind, and strength into the principle "God loves." Indeed, according to this passage, if you want to know what love is, look at God's nature and actions, not at what people do.

Farther along in the same passage, this early interpreter of the Gospel of John says that love is God's own nature: "God is love" (1 John 4:16). The word "love" has ceased to be a commandment and become, instead, a word interchangeable with the word "God." This means that love is the first principle of the universe; love is what holds the world together and makes it run. Have the author of the Gospel of John and the early interpreter who wrote 1 John thrown out Deuteronomy 6:4-5, stood it on its head, interpreted it out of existence? No, I don't think so. I think we have a meditation on Deuteronomy 6:4-5, in which the word "love" that occurs in verse 5 has come to dominate verse 4 as well. I think these authors have read Deuteronomy 6:4-5 as though it said,"Hear, O Israel, the Lord your God is love; and you shall love the Lord your God with all your heart, and with all your soul, and with all your might" (Deuteronomy 6:4-5, altered). In other words, they have read "love" where the Bible says "one" in the statement about the nature of God which is the basis for the commandment to love God. Did you notice that the prayer in John 17 also keeps the ideas of "unity" and "love" close together? There the unity of the church is based on mutual love; here the nature of God, which is usually spoken of as "unity," is described as "love."

There is only one more step in our excursion through the world of the love commandment as it is interpreted by the Gospel of John and explained by 1 John. That step is to ask how the two commandments, Deuteronomy 6:4-5 and Leviticus 19:18, work together. Once again 1 John gives us a quotable quote: "Beloved, if God so loved us, we also ought to love one another" (1 John 4:11). God's love, which is prior to any action we take, calls forth the response of love among Christians. In our excursion through the world of the love commandment, we have met the idea of the priority of God's love and the idea of love as response over and over again. In chapter 2 we looked at Deuteronomy 7:8-9. Let me pick out just a few words to remind you that this meditation on Deuteronomy 6:4-5 and Leviticus 19:18 and on their relationship echoes old themes. "It is because the LORD loves you . . . that the LORD . . . redeemed you . . . Know therefore that the LORD your God is . . . the faithful God who keeps covenant and steadfast love with those who love him . . . to a thousand generations" (Deuteronomy 7:8-9).

We have seen how the early interpreter of the Gospel of John who wrote 1 John defends not using "love" to describe the response to God. We need also to note, in considering how the two commandments work together, that the symmetry of the two commandments, Deuteronomy 6:4-5 and Leviticus 19:18, brings the term back in spite of this:

> We love, because he first loved us. If anyone says, "I love God," and hates his brother, he is a liar; for he who does not love his brother whom he has seen, cannot love God whom he has not seen. And this commandment we have from him, that he who loves God should love his brother also (1 John 4:19-21).

Here this author betrays knowledge that there is a commandment that reads "You shall love . . . God" (Deuteronomy 6:5). Even though it may seem inappropriate to use the same word for your response to God that you use for your response to other Christians, the idea of the priority of God's love demands a symmetrical response—to God and to Christians. Using the word "love" for both responses maintains that symmetry nicely.

The Gospel of John is often called the "spiritual" Gospel. From what does its peculiar religious intensity come? And what does its peculiar religious intensity have to do with the religious intensity we have found wherever Jesus' love commandment is interpreted? The religious intensity of the Gospel of John comes from making Christ present in the church. The portrayal of Jesus makes him transparent to God, so that wherever Jesus is, God is present in power. Future events of salvation, such as the resurrection, leave the future and become present wherever Jesus goes. The presence of Christ in the church is so real, in the Gospel of John, that he can be said to make his home there.

I am always struck by the fact that Jesus gives only one commandment in John: "Love one another." Nothing else. Relations between church members are not just social, lived out at the level of human interaction; they participate in the life of God and in a love which is divine. To participate in church activities is, for the Gospel of John, to live with Christ. The intense mutuality of a close Christian fellowship is itself the locus of the religious intensity Mark's scribe exhibited when he concentrated his attention on God alone.

7

Paul's Interpretation

The last stage of our tour of the world of the love commandment takes us into a new and different kind of terrain. Here there are no stories about Jesus, no speeches by Jesus. Jesus will scarcely appear on the horizon, much less step forward to command. Our tour takes us, now, through the letters of Paul.

Paul was the first author of a New Testament book. Of course, he didn't set out to write books to put in a Bible. He wrote because he needed to and said what he needed to say to the people he addressed. Paul wrote letters when he was too far away to pay a visit in person. What he said in his letters depended on the situation. Sometimes he filled in the gaps in the knowledge of these new Christians; sometimes he answered questions they raised by letter or messenger; sometimes he corrected errors; several times he wrote to encourage contributions to the fund he was assembling for the church in Jerusalem.

There are few stories in Paul's letters, but each of the letters is part of a story. Reading one of Paul's letters is like listening to one side of a telephone conversation. You can discern something of who is at the other end of the line and what is on their mind, but you can't hear what they are saying and sometimes you miss the point entirely. There is a story here, and reading Paul's letters gives you half of it plus a few tantalizing glimpses of the other half.

Because we often don't know much about the story in which the letter belongs, a letter by Paul may seem very general. It may look like an article in a church magazine on some topic of faith or life. In such cases it resembles an essay, designed to explore some aspect of the Christian faith, analyze it, and apply it to Christian living. In some ways essays are easier to understand than stories. Certainly it is easier to argue with an essay than with a story. The author will give reasons, define the terms, and defend a thesis. If you disagree, you can think of reasons why the thesis doesn't hold water or the advice is irrelevant to any sensible assessment of the world.

One of the things we don't know about Paul is what Paul knew about Jesus. Certainly Paul knew about Jesus' crucifixion and resurrection. He talks about it frequently. But it is difficult to know what Paul knew about Jesus' ministry, his teachings, the stories he told, the healing of sick people, the table fellowship with disciples. When our tour takes us into this area, we find ourselves on rough roads through fascinating territory with few landmarks.

Did Paul know that Jesus had quoted Deuteronomy 6:4-5 and Leviticus 19:18 and made them the basic principle of intellectual and moral life? Did Paul know anything at all similar to what we know about the love commandment? Paul couldn't have read the stories we have read in Matthew, Mark, Luke, and John because none of those books, not even Mark, had yet been written. He might have heard some of the stories told in sermons. Which ones? In what form? This is unmarked territory we are entering. Our only maps to the territory, the only clues to Paul's interpretation of the love commandment, are Paul's letters and what they say.

Touring Corinthians

We turn now to Paul's letters. If I were to ask any group of Christians for directions for finding what Paul says about love, quite a number of people would direct me to 1 Corinthians 13. Surely 1 Corinthians 13 ranks among the all-time favorite passages of Scripture, right up there with the Twenty-third Psalm and the Christmas story. We might as well begin there.

First Corinthians 13 is lodged firmly between 1 Corinthians 12 and 1 Corinthians 14, and the three chapters make up a unit. The Christians in Corinth had trouble in their church. They submitted to Paul their quarrels and the questions which divided them. Some questions were written in a letter; others were asked in person by messengers who came to see Paul. In the letter we call 1 Corinthians, Paul takes up one at a time the issues raised by the church in Corinth, and gives a clear signal each time he takes up a new topic. Here are some of the signals: "Now concerning the matters about which you wrote" (1 Corinthians 7:1). What follows in chapter 7 is a discussion of marriage and associated issues. Then comes "Now concerning food offered to idols" (1 Corinthians 8:1), followed by a discussion of that issue and some others. Then comes "Now concerning spiritual gifts" (1 Corinthians 12:1) and a discussion in chapters 12 through 14 of the use of spiritual gifts in worship. Many books, essays and pamphlets of Paul's day bore titles beginning "Now concerning. . . ." It was a fashionable way to title a work, and I have no doubt that Paul's first readers picked up the clue about the beginning and ending of a passage. Now we know something about the context of 1 Corinthians 13: It is part of Paul's solution to an argument about using spiritual gifts in worship.

Some people have doubted that 1 Corinthians 13 really belongs with chapters 12 and 14, considering it to be pasted in by a later editor. They point to the contrasts. First, chapters 12 and 14 are prose like the rest of the letter; chapter 13 is poetry, or a hymn, or something like that. Second, chapters 12 and 14 are about the specifics of arranging the church; chapter 13 is very general, saying poetic and philosophical things that apply to many situations. Third, worship relates people to God; love relates people to each other. Some of these interpreters think Paul could not possibly have written a poem as beautiful as 1 Corinthians 13. There is no reason, in my opinion, to think Paul was incapable of writing poetry. I know all kinds of people with hidden talents. The fact that someone usually writes prose doesn't prove she can't write poetry on occasion. The contrasts also fail to convince me that the three chapters don't belong together. Here is the evidence that 1 Corinthians 13 belongs with 1 Corinthians 12 and 14.

The spiritual gift that is causing the problem in Corinth is "speaking in tongues." Speaking in tongues means saying words no one understands, under the direct influence of the Holy Spirit. Paul's definition of speaking in tongues in 1 Corinthians 14 is "one who speaks in a tongue speaks not to men but to God; for no one understands him, but he utters mysteries in the Spirit" (1 Corinthians 14:2).

Paul also talks about speaking in tongues in chapter 13, using the poetic phrase "tongues of angels." The first section of 1 Corinthians 13, verses 1-3, contrasts "love" to a variety of religious gifts, claiming that none is complete without love: "If I speak in the tongues of men and of angels, but have not love, I am a noisy gong or a clanging cymbal" (1 Corinthians 13:1). That the first item to which love is contrasted is precisely the topic of chapters 12 and 14 sends me a message that chapter 13 belongs with chapter 12 and 14.

The second section of 1 Corinthians 13, verses 4-7, lists the virtues love possesses, beginning with "Love is patient and kind" (1 Corinthians 13:4). This section doesn't apply love to any situation, such as speaking in tongues. Rather, it enumerates the excellences of love.

The last section of 1 Corinthians 13, verses 8-13, contrasts things that are imperfect, partial, or temporary, belonging to our ordinary experience, with things that are perfect, complete, and permanent, belonging to the future reign of God. Where does love fit in? "Love never ends; as for prophecies, they will pass away; as for tongues, they will cease; as for knowledge, it will pass away" (1 Corinthians 13:8). Once again, love is superior to every good thing you can think of. It is the thing that belongs both to here and to hereafter, a bit of heaven on earth. That "love" is contrasted to "tongues," the topic that Paul discusses in chapters 12 and 14, tells me for the second time that 1 Corinthians 13 belongs with the two chapters surrounding it.

Paul has written a beautiful poem focusing our attention on love, something which he displays as being of the highest value. I think he has done what, in the sentence before 1 Corinthians 13 begins, he said that he intended to do, "I will show you a still more excellent way" (1 Corinthians 12:31). But what does he expect his readers to do with the excellences he has set before us? He himself proposes an answer in the sentence just after 1 Corinthians 13, "Make love your aim" (1 Corinthians 14:1). What he says in 1 Corinthians 14 is a demonstration of how to aim at love. It is, to put it another way, application of love to the matter at hand, in this case a particular problem of the use and abuse of speaking in tongues during worship services.

Does Paul's speech in praise of love remind you of the love commandment as we have seen it so far? The word "love" is present, to be sure, but where is the quotation of Deuteronomy 6:4-5 and Leviticus 19:18? Making love the key to the right interpretation of various things reminds me of Matthew's interpretation of the love commandment. Matthew, you recall, thinks Jesus made the love commandment the key to Scripture. In the first part of the Sermon on the Mount, Matthew shows how Jesus interpreted Scripture, using love to clarify and to sharpen the focus of various passages of the Old Testament. Paul, it seems to me, does something similar. He makes love the criterion for analyzing social situations and for solving problems such as priorities in arrangements for worship. When he makes love the criterion for right worship, Paul makes me think of Mark's interpretation of the love commandment. The scribe in Mark, you recall, thought the love commandment authorized a preference for spiritual worship over animal sacrifice. Here there is nothing about animal sacrifice, of course, but certainly the issue is the right way to organize spiritual worship. Finally, when Paul describes love as permanent he reminds me of the Gospel of John. In John, as here, there is no quotation of the basic Old Testament passages. Also in John, as here, we have poetic meditations. In John we find "abide in my love" (John 15:9); here Paul concludes his praise of love with the words, "So faith, hope, love abide, these three; but the greatest of these is love" (1 Corinthians 13:13). I am sure there is a difference between "love abides" and "abiding in love," but at this point I am more struck by the similarity than by the difference.

Did Paul know, when he wrote 1 Corinthians 13, that Jesus had quoted Deuteronomy 6:4-5 and Leviticus 19:18 and made them of the greatest importance? Paul doesn't say what he knows. But what he says overlaps to a remarkable extent with what we have seen in our tours of the other New Testament interpretations of the love commandment. Whatever Paul knew, it is legitimate because of the similarities for us to interpret 1 Corinthians 13 as a meditation on the love commandment.

There are places in his letters where Paul quotes Leviticus 19:18. We will look at his letter to the Galatians first and then at his letter to the Romans.

Touring Galatians

We don't know quite what it was that turned the Christians in Galatia against Paul. All we know is what Paul tells us and the way he tells it. Here is the story as best we can construct it from Paul's letter. Apparently some non-Jewish Christian did something that was very, very wrong by any conceivable standard. Then some other Christians argued that if only all Christians would bind themselves to obey the Old Testament law they would know what to do and what not to do. A good first step, so this argument went, would be for all non-Jewish Christians to be circumsised. It is at this point that Paul enters the story. He considers any such argument to be an attack on the gospel he preaches, and he proceeds to defend the gospel like a lawyer defending a client. He even organizes his letter like a speech written to defend a client in open court. If, when the Christians in Galatia received the letter, they had someone read it aloud in church, the reader would be like a lawyer reading a speech in defense of the gospel, and the congregation would be asked to make a decision about the gospel, like a jury deciding a case in court.

In chapter 5 and the first part of chapter 6 Paul argues that the issue is as clear as the choice between freedom and slavery: "For freedom Christ has set us free; stand fast therefore, and do not submit again to a yoke of slavery"

(Galatians 5:1). The slavery Paul is anxious for the Christians to avoid is slavery to circumcision and with it to the whole of Old Testament law. He explains: "For in Christ Jesus neither circumcision nor uncircumcision is of any avail, but faith working through love" (Galatians 5:6).

Now we can see his argument more clearly. The slavery he is talking about is a slavery to things that have nothing to do with salvation and the Christian life, things like circumcision and uncircumcision. The freedom he is talking about is freedom to concentrate on what matters for Christian faith and Christian life. He uses the phrase "faith working through love" to define "freedom." In the first half of chapter 5, then, Paul has argued that Christian freedom involves a lifestyle characterized by "love."

In the second half of chapter 5, Paul describes the way love governs Christian life:

> For you were called to freedom, brethren; only do not use your freedom as an opportunity for the flesh, but through love be servants of one another. For the whole law is fulfilled in one word, "You shall love your neighbor as yourself" (Galatians 5:13-14).

Here at last we have a quotation of Leviticus 19:18. We should pause to inspect how Paul uses it. It appears, at the beginning, that there is a right way and a wrong way to use freedom. The wrong way to use freedom is called "an opportunity for the flesh"; the right way is stated as a commandment, "be servants of one another."

Right here we see an apparent contradiction. Didn't Paul just get through denouncing a yoke of slavery to law in verse one? Why is he giving a new law, "be servants of one another"? Isn't this a case of pushing law out the front door only to have it sneak in the back door?

Let's look at the argument Paul makes in these two verses. His general principle is Leviticus 19:18, "You shall love your neighbor as yourself." "Through love be servants of one another" is Paul's paraphrase of Leviticus 19:18, a paraphrase which connects the general principle to the situation at hand, the use of freedom. From these two verses alone we can learn two important things about Paul's interpretation of the love commandment. First, Paul thinks that Leviticus 19:18 is a general principle which undergirds the whole of Christian life. Leviticus 19:18 renders the whole apparatus of Old Testament law, from circumcision on, as an unnecessary and enslaving burden, according to Paul's interpretation in this letter. In this respect, Paul agrees with the scribe in Mark and with Jesus in Luke. Second, Paul thinks that "You shall love your neighbor as yourself" means mutual and reciprocal love among Christians, "through love be servants of one another." In this respect Paul agrees with the author of the Gospel of John that Jesus gave only one law and that was to "love one another."

Farther down the road in this chapter, Paul makes two lists, in which he contrasts "the works of the flesh" with "the fruit of the Spirit." The first item on the list under the title "fruit of the Spirit" is "love." Now we can see something more of what Paul meant in verse 6 by the phrase "faith working through love." Paul has the idea that, when you have faith in Jesus Christ, the Holy Spirit works in you. What the Spirit does is "bear fruit" in you, and the fruit is both something you do and something done through you. From your point of view, the fruit of the Spirit is a gift to you, and whatever you do in love is not a burdensome chore. Indeed, it is hardly even something *you* do at all. So, in Paul's view "be servants of one another" is not a chore to be done but a description of how the Spirit bears fruit. If the fruit of the Spirit is love, we can hardly avoid being servants of one another, unless we resist the Spirit or refuse the gift.

At the beginning of chapter 6, in verses 1 through 10, Paul describes a problem situation and advises the Galatians about how to deal with it:

> Brethren, if a man is overtaken in any trespass, you who are spiritual should restore him in a spirit of gentleness. Look to yourself, lest you too be tempted. Bear one another's burdens, and so fulfil the law of Christ (Galatians 6:1-2).

I suspect that the case Paul describes with the general words "if a man is overtaken in any trespass" was not a hypothetical case. I believe it was well known in all its gossipy details to the Christians to whom the letter is addressed. We who live many centuries later don't need to know much more about the circumstances of the case. What we need to observe is how Paul thinks such a situation should be dealt with. Should such a person be kicked out of the church? The technical term is "excommunication." No, says Paul, the goal is not to get rid of him but to restore him. The most important things Paul has to say here are about how to restore this person. Let's look at what Paul proposes.

First of all, Paul thinks restoring a member who has strayed off the moral path is a job for the leadership of the congregation, "you who are spiritual." It is a job which poses spiritual dangers to those involved and requires a mature self-awareness. The most significant danger, the one Paul points to, is the danger of getting a big head, of deceiving yourself that you are immune to fouling up your life in the same or some other way. "For if any one thinks he is something, when he is nothing, he deceives himself" (Galatians 6:3). It is indeed difficult to maintain a sense that "we're all in this together" when dealing with people who are in trouble clear up to their ears, as professionals in social services, corrections, health care, education, and other helping professions know very well. The big spiritual danger for all such people is spiritual pride.

Second, Paul states a general principle to guide the process of restoring with gentleness, a principle which takes into account both the trespasser and the church leadership. That principle is: "Bear one another's burdens and so fulfil the law of Christ." Clearly, this is another paraphrase of Leviticus 19:18, "You shall love your neighbor as yourself," which shows how Leviticus 19:18 applies to the situation at hand. Here, for the first time, Paul calls Leviticus 19:18 "the law of Christ." Now we can be sure that Paul knew Jesus had quoted Leviticus 19:18 and had made it a general principle of moral life that stands out above any others.

Third, to understand what Paul means, you have to be willing to interpret Leviticus 19:18 as if it said, "Love one another." The words "one another," indicating mutuality, are very important to Paul. In this case, Paul wants the leaders of the congregration to regard the burden of the trespass as something to share. The sharing is designed to keep it from being too heavy a burden for any one person, either for the trespasser himself, the one who bears the ultimate responsibility, or for any single leader, for whom bearing someone else's burden might constitute a temptation to spiritual pride. Notice that there is no second step in restoring the trespasser to the reciprocal relationship of Christian love in the church. It is not a matter of bearing his burden first and then, after that, restoring him to full fellowship. No, to share his burden is to include him in the church again.

It may be helpful to recall at this point our observation in chapter 2 that Leviticus 19:18, in its original setting, commanded treating strangers and foreigners the way you wished to be treated when you were strangers and foreigners. Some early Christians interpreted it precisely this way. For example, in Matthew we found it applied to "enemies," and in Luke we found a story dealing with a Samaritan who was both a foreigner and an enemy. Other early Christians applied "You shall love your neighbor as yourself" to relations within the Christian community. The Gospel of John did this, formulating Leviticus 19:18 as "Love one another," and Paul does the same thing here. I think the Gospel of John intended to limit the application of Leviticus 19:18 to mutual relations in the church. There are few clues as to whether Paul is doing the same thing or whether he is just limiting himself to talking about the situation before him. We need to be alert to those clues.

Before we leave Galatians, we need to look at the organization of Galatians 6:1-10. In inspecting the first verses, we located the general principle "Bear one another's burdens and so fulfil the law of Christ." Before that was the description of the situation and a formula for resolving it. We also found a statement of concern for the church leaders, "Look to yourself." Following the general principle is a discussion, in verses 3-5, of the danger to church leaders and, in verses 7-9, of the ultimate responsibility before God of the trespasser for whatever it is he has done, including "whatever a man sows, that he will also reap" (Galatians 6:7). The passage ends with two admonitions to do good even in discouraging circumstances. The second is: "So then, as we have opportunity, let us do good to all men, and especially to those who are of the household of faith" (Galatians 6:10). In this admonition Paul appears not to limit his concern to relations within the church, even though that is his primary concern in this and many other passages.

Touring Romans

The other place where Paul discusses the love commandment is in his letter to the Romans. This is the last stop on our tour of Paul's interpretation of the love commandment, and one of the most complicated. Paul had never been to Rome, and the letter he wrote to the church there was intended to introduce himself and to announce his plans for a visit. Because the Romans did not know Paul, he wrote for them some examples of his theology and the gospel he preached, putting his best foot forward. Because Paul didn't know the Romans directly, and perhaps because grapevines are notoriously unreliable sources of information in any age, Paul doesn't write to respond to crises in Rome or to questions from Rome. It is possible to put Paul's letter to the Romans into a story involving their church and Paul's overall mission, but it isn't necessary for most purposes, including ours. It would have been difficult to understand why Paul said what he said to the Corinthians and the Galatians without attempting first to understand the problems those churches faced. Not so, Romans. We will find it easy enough to approach the love commandment in Romans without knowing the situation with any precision.

We begin our tour of Paul's interpretation of the love commandment for the Romans with the place where Leviticus 19:18 appears:

> Owe no one anything, except to love one another; for he who loves his neighbor has fulfilled the law. The commandments, "You shall not commit adultery, You shall not kill, You shall not steal, You shall not covet," and any other commandment, are summed up in this sentence, "You shall love your neighbor as yourself." Love does no wrong to a neighbor; therefore love is the fulfilling of the law (Romans 13:8-10).

The passage quoted from Paul's letter to the Romans is composed of three sections. In the first section Paul treats "love one another" as a command to love your neighbor. He does not think of neighbor as an outsider or a foreigner, as the Old Testament does, and he does not eliminate the term "neighbor" in favor of "each other" as the Gospel of John does. Clearly, in Paul's day there was no discussion about how wide a circle of people ought to be loved.

The second section of our quotation lists several of the Ten Commandments and says that Leviticus 19:18 summarizes them. Here, as in Matthew, Leviticus 19:18 is the key to interpreting Scripture.

The third section shows the love commandment as the clue to correct social behavior and ethical living. Here the love commandment means not doing wrong to a neighbor. We don't know whether Paul knew the story of the good Samaritan, with its surprising use of the foreigner as a model of ethical living and its use of ethical living as a clue to salvation, but he does echo the same themes.

I find the three-part paragraph we are looking at odd. Paul heaps up phrases as though he wanted to call our attention to something. But what? It reminds me of the conclusion to a symphony, the kind that builds up to a climax and then starts over again to build up to yet another climax. Where, I want to know, is the symphony to which Romans 13:8-10 is the ending? Let's look around. If Romans 13:8-10 is the end of something, where is the beginning?

Everyone who reads Romans notices that a new section begins at the beginning of Romans 12. In addition, the word "love" appears in Romans 12:9. So, I propose that we investigate Romans 12:1—13:10 as an essay on the love commandment.

> I appeal to you therefore, brethren, by the mercies of God, to present your bodies as a living sacrifice, holy and acceptable to God, which is your spiritual worship. Do not be conformed to this world but be transformed by the renewal of your mind, that you may prove what is the will of God, what is good and acceptable and perfect (Romans 12:1-2).

The first two verses of our passage have a large number of words that have to do with worship. To begin with, there is the phrase "spiritual worship." Then there are the words for sacrifice, "present your bodies as a living sacrifice." An animal suitable for sacrifice would be one which is "good and acceptable and perfect." Clearly, this is no description of a worship service involving human sacrifices. No blood will be shed here. The furnishings of the place of worship do not include a knife or a basin to catch blood. Rather, this whole passage speaks in metaphors. This worship is "spiritual" worship; this sacrifice is a "living" sacrifice. The bodies to be presented are the self-presentations of the worshipers. Bodies, so dedicated, join renewed minds to make up selves which are said to be "transformed."

These two verses have always made me think of Deuteronomy 6:4-5, especially the way Mark interprets it. The scribe in Mark, you will remember, thought loving God with all your inner faculties was "much more than all whole burnt offerings and sacrifices" (Mark 12:33). Clearly, Paul also considers worship as an inward act of total devotion. Where the scribe, echoing Jesus and Deuteronomy 6:4-5, described that total devotion with the categories of heart, understanding, and strength, Paul uses the categories of body and mind.

Paul differs from the scribe in Mark when he uses the category "body," because body is not an inner source or capacity. Body always takes up space, is always public, always engages the outside world. Paul's interpretation guards carefully against a worship so spiritual that it makes no outward, earthly difference. Indeed, the phrases he uses to talk about mind do something of the same thing. He speaks of a "renewal" of the mind which transforms the total self. The spiritual worship Paul speaks of makes a difference in the world.

The acid test of spiritual worship, according to these two verses, is producing people who know what the will of God is. When Paul says "that you may prove what is the will of God," he doesn't mean "prove" as in a mathematical proof, and he doesn't mean "prove" as in proving a Christian case to a skeptical, non-Christian world. He means having a sure instinct for moral distinctions. What Christians, transformed by the renewal of their minds, will do is to sort through the moral options and the possible lifestyles and choose what is acceptable to God.

Paul's interpretation of Deuteronomy 6:4-5 says what the scribe in Mark says; i.e., intense and total concentration directly and exclusively on God alone. But Paul's interpretation goes beyond that of the scribe, because he sees the connection of worship to life. The scribe in Mark quoted Leviticus 19:18 in answer to Jesus but didn't get excited about it. Paul, by contrast, who quotes neither Deuteronomy 6:4-5 nor Leviticus 19:18, seems to me to prescribe for spiritual worship not only the total and exclusive concentration on God that belongs to Deuteronomy 6:4-5, but also a public and social character that belongs to Leviticus 19:18.

Our tour of Romans 12:1—13:10 has taken us through the last three verses and the first two verses so far. We have located the end of the passage, Romans 13:8-10, which quotes Leviticus 19:18, and we have located the beginning of the passage, Romans 12:1-2, which interprets Deuteronomy

6:4-5 in somewhat the same way the scribe in Mark interpreted it, but without quoting the passage. Between these we should find an interpretation of Leviticus 19:18, one that ends in 13:8-10 with quoting the verse itself.

> For by the grace given to me I bid every one among you not to think of himself more highly than he ought to think, but to think with sober judgment, each according to the measure of faith which God has assigned him (Romans 12:3).

When Paul writes an essay he often puts a major idea at the beginning and then repeats it in other, sometimes clearer, terms at the end. If that is the case here, we should be able to find something like "You shall love your neighbor as yourself" in Romans 12:3.

The opposite of what Paul will urge in this essay, the error to be avoided, appears in the first phrases, "I bid every one among you not to think of himself more highly than he ought to think." Having an inflated idea of your own importance was what Paul warned against in Galatians 6, wasn't it? There he spoke of spiritual pride as thinking you are "something" when you are "nothing"; here he speaks of spiritual pride as thinking of yourself "more highly than [you] ought to think." In Galatians, the opposite of spiritual pride was bearing one another's burdens. Here the opposite of spiritual pride is "think with sober judgment . . . according to the measure of faith." What does thinking with sober judgment according to the measure of faith have to do with Leviticus 19:18?

Thinking with sober judgment could be the kind of thinking required for interpreting scripture with Leviticus 19:18 as the key. If so, Romans 12:3 is indeed the beginning of something for which Romans 13:9 is the end. On the other hand, "thinking with sober judgment" is a general phrase and probably could be applied to many things other than interpreting Scripture. In that case, the connection between this phrase and anything in 13:8-10 is not very strong.

Let's look now at the phrase "measure of faith." What does "measure of faith" mean? I used to think of it as a calibrated measuring cup to measure some quantity of faith. Then I had to worry about whether God had given me enough faith for making sober judgments. The problem with this kind of thinking is that faith isn't something you have a little or a lot of. Earlier in his letter to the Romans, Paul uses "faith" and "believe" in his usual way, "the righteousness of God through faith in Jesus Christ for all who believe" (Romans 3:22). For Paul there is an absolute difference between "believing" and "not believing," between "faith" and "not faith." After you once confess your faith in Jesus Christ, you grow in Christian maturity, but you don't acquire an additional amount of faith. It's like pregnancy. Once you are pregnant you don't get more pregnant; you just get bigger. If "measure of faith" isn't anything like a measuring cup to measure how much faith you have, what kind of measuring device is it, and what, after all, does it measure?

I think Paul was thinking of a much simpler measuring device than a measuring cup, one that gives only a "yes" or "no." Perhaps a plumb line would be a good example. When you drop a plumb line from the top of a wall, you find out whether the wall leans or goes straight up. You don't get any other information from the plumb line. To measure how far it leans, you need another instrument. I use the word "criterion" for a simple device that tells you "yes" or "no." If you apply such a criterion to your judgment, it will tell you only whether your judgment is sober or frivolous and inflated.

What criterion does Paul propose that we use to tell us whether we are thinking of ourselves more highly than we ought to think or whether, alternatively, we are thinking with sound judgment? Paul doesn't identify his criterion in Romans 12:3 at the beginning of the discussion. But he does identify it at the end in 13:9. The criterion for making a Christian sober judgment is "You shall love your neighbor as yourself."

Now we know that Romans 12:3—13:9 is, indeed, a discussion of the love commandment, despite the fact that neither the word "love," nor Leviticus 19:18, nor a paraphrase appears in 12:3. We need to look rather briefly at the way Paul organizes his discussion of the love commandment here, if only because of its resemblances to other interpretations of the love commandment.

Paul proceeds in Romans 12:4-8 to define sober judgment according to the criterion of love. He does so by recourse to the image of the body: "For as in one body we have many members, and all the members do not have the same function, so we, though many, are one body in Christ, and individually members one of another" (Romans 12:4-5). Paul used the image of the body in 1 Corinthians 12 to talk about mutuality and reciprocity. There he followed it with his praise of the excellences of love in chapter 13. Here the image is repeated with the same associations. Once again the image of the body helps him to show how interdependent we are; it interprets the words "as yourself" in Leviticus 19:18 or "one another" in the paraphrase "love one another."

The next section, Romans 12:9-21, consists of little short phrases: "Let love be genuine; hate what is evil, hold fast to what is good; love one another with brotherly affection; outdo one another in showing honor" (Romans 12:9-10). It continues in this vein. I have quoted enough to give you the flavor. The first line contains a problem for translators. Let me explain. The sentence in Greek consists of only two words:

1. "Love"
2. "Genuine"

Since you can't have a sentence in English without a verb, the translators had to put in some form of the verb "to be." They had the choice of making the sentence a description, "Love *is* genuine" or a command "*Let* love *be* genuine." I think they chose the wrong one.

Many of the verbs which follow in Greek are participles. Greek participles are sometimes translated into English as commands; more often they are translated as adjectives. In this case, they could be translated as adjectives describing genuine love. If my two suggestions for translation were adopted the passage would begin: "Love is genuine, hating what is evil, loving one another with brotherly affection, outdoing one another in showing honor." I have taken this small detour through these matters of translation for a reason. There is a strong resemblance, it seems to me, between these verses and the description of love in 1 Corinthians 13:4-5, "Love is patient and kind; love is not jealous or boastful; it is not arrogant or rude." I think that Paul is describing love in the same way to the Romans as he had described it to the Corinthians: first, a discussion using the image of the body to demonstrate mutuality and interdependence; second, a direct description of love using short phrases.

There are several interesting features of Romans 12:9-21 which tell us something about Paul's interpretation of the love commandment. The first is that while almost all the phrases in verses 9-13 are about relations within the church, verse 14 deals with persecutors, and the verses which follow are mostly about other relations to people outside the church. It looks to me as though Paul intends to say that the love commandment is the criterion for Christian life, not only in the church but also with those outside the church.

The second feature of Romans 12:9-21 which is important for a tour of the world of the love commandment has to do with dealing with enemies:

> Beloved, never avenge yourselves, but leave it to the wrath of God; for it is written, "Vengeance is mine, I will repay, says the Lord." No, "if your enemy is hungry, feed him; if he is thirsty, give him drink; for by so doing you will heap burning coals upon his head." Do not be overcome by evil, but overcome evil with good (Romans 12:19-21).

Comparisons with both Matthew's and Luke's interpretation come to mind. Matthew, you will recall, has Jesus demonstrate how the love commandment functions to remove all limitations to the application of Old Testament law.

> You have heard that it was said, "You shall love your neighbor and hate your enemy." But I say to you, Love your enemies and pray for those who persecute you (Matthew 5:43-44).

Paul does seem to have the same idea, doesn't he? He has already said in this discussion of the love commandment, "Bless those who persecute you; bless and do not curse them" (Romans 12:14). Here he brings together two bits from the Old Testament, Deuteronomy 32:35 and Proverbs 25:21-22, to show how to love one's neighbor in situations where hostility can't be resolved or avoided. Let me summarize his sentences as two rules: (1) No retaliation; (2) Positive actions of hospitality.

Much has been said about what kinds of positive actions ought to be undertaken to love an enemy. You can read the thought developed by Gandhi and adapted to the American situation by Martin Luther King, Jr., for example, and you can read stories and manuals about the practice of nonviolence. Most such thought about nonviolent direct action begins with Matthew 5 and the similar material in Luke 6. To my way of thinking, Paul has similar and quite specific ideas. What do you do to love an enemy? Here is Paul's reply: First, renounce vengeance; Second, provide for basic needs, practicing hospitality toward hostile persons.

Underlying both rules I gleaned from Romans 12:19-21 is the notion of handing the whole hostile situation over to God, a notion Paul expresses by quoting "leave it to the wrath of God" and "by so doing you will heap burning coals upon his head." No one knows quite what the figure of speech "heaping burning coals on someone's head" means. Perhaps it meant something like our figure of speech "to hand someone a hot potato," which means—am I correct here?—to leave them in a dilemma, some difficult situation which requires quick action and which probably has no solution that is both dignified and wholly satisfactory. The idea, in any case, is that the burden of the hostility is no longer yours; it is a matter between your enemy and God. Isn't that what Jesus had in mind, according to Matthew 5? In praying for your enemy you leave the hostile situation in God's hands. This implies that any remaining hostility is a matter between your enemy and God, though the implication isn't spelled out in Matthew as it is here.

Romans 12:19-21 can also be compared to Luke's interpretation of the love commandment. Who, in all the stories in the whole New Testament, is more famous for providing for the basic needs of an enemy than the good Samaritan? You could almost imagine that the Samaritan took Romans 12:19-21 as a recipe! And what, from the victim's point of view, was the result? Getting help from an unwanted source made the victim pretty uncomfortable, didn't it? And Jesus told the parable, we recall, in answer to a question about inheriting eternal life. I am impressed by the similarity between this part of Paul's interpretation of the love commandment and Luke's. Paul, I think, would explain the parable of the good Samaritan this way. When practical hospitality was practiced toward him by an enemy, the victim was left in a dilemma: the enmity no longer existed between victim and Samaritan; it was a matter between victim and God, who wills salvation. In accepting the hospitality of an enemy, the victim found salvation.

We have arrived at the end of chapter 12, but the end of the section is still quite a way down the road. Romans 13:1-7 is a paragraph, complete in itself, about Christian relations with government officials, beginning, "Let every person be subject to the governing authorities." It is a problem paragraph. Some people think Paul didn't write it at all because it is so enthusiastic about Roman rule and seems to approve of everything the Roman Empire does, without qualification and without careful inspection. Other people are quite sure, for the very same reasons, that Paul did write it. No one I know thinks it has anything to do with loving your neighbor. The passage has been used, over the centuries, to urge Christians to obey their governments without question and without hesitation. I am quite certain that all governments need critical inspection by Christian citizens and that this passage has been used to shelter evil plans and projects from public scrutiny. I also think that the passage is better than its uses. It is a basic statement of early Christian political philosophy, whether by Paul or by someone else, and should be analyzed as ancient political philosophy. We could take a detour off the path of our tour through Paul's interpretation of the love commandment to evaluate it, but I think we should pass up the opportunity and hurry along. Someone, at any rate, whether Paul or some later editor of Paul's letters, decided to put the paragraph here, sandwiched between Paul's best thought on dealing with enemies, Romans 12:19-21, and his summary and conclusion of the discussion of the love commandment, Romans 13:8-10. That says to me that someone thought that, for situations where your neighbor is not an individual or a small group, you need a political philosophy in order to love your neighbor correctly. If your neighbor is the Roman Empire, for example, or the Internal

Revenue Service or the City of Des Moines, you need some systematic idea of the sources and limits of political power and governmental prerogative. We have here Paul's ideas on such subjects, or those attributed to him.

We arrive finally, at the conclusion to Paul's essay on the love commandment, Romans 13:8-10. When we quoted it and discussed it at the beginning, we thought it was like the conclusion to a symphony. Now we have located the whole symphony. Paul has written a tightly organized essay on the love commandment. Here is the outline, a summary of what we have seen:

Interpretation of Deuteronomy 6:4-5	12:1-2
Interpretation of Leviticus 19:18	12:3—13:10
Principle: Criterion of Christian faith is love	12:3
Explanation of "as yourself": parts of body	12:4-8
Description of love: It is genuine	12:9-21
—within the church	12:9-13
—in relation to outsiders	12:14-21
—the special case of civil authorities	13:1-7
Conclusion	13:8-10

Paul has interpreted both Deuteronomy 6:4-5 and Leviticus 19:18 with great care and in great detail. We have seen elsewhere that he thinks of the love commandment as the law of Christ. Here we see him taking it with the seriousness appropriate to Christ's law and finding in it many of the things Matthew, Mark, Luke, and John heard in what Jesus said.

8

How to Find the Meaning for Today

The subtitle of this book furnishes the title for this chapter. But there is more reason for this chapter than an excuse to use the subtitle of the book. While you are on a scenic tour of the landscape and architecture of the New Testament, the highways and byways, antechambers, and pavilions of the earliest Christian literature, you can put your own world on hold, set your own problems on the back burner to simmer by themselves, sit back, and enjoy the ride. This isn't escapism. We all know what escapist books are like, and they aren't much like this one. Rather, this has been a planned excursion, a departure from the everyday, undertaken for the sake of returning to the everyday. In this chapter we return to the everyday, and it is when we return that the question arises: What does it all mean?

We have taken an extended tour of a multiple text, a text which is an interpretation of an interpretation of an interpretation. As we approached the end of our tour we spent as much time comparing one interpretation to another as we did inspecting the interpretation at hand. This multiple text has become, in the later stages of our tour, a multiple text in three dimensions. It isn't so simple a matter as seeing Jesus interpreting two verses from the Old Testament and then seeing five separate and independent interpretations of Jesus' interpretation of the Old Testament. That would be complicated enough. The matter is more complicated because some interpreters, such as Matthew and Luke, interpret other interpretations (Mark) in addition to that of Jesus and, as is the case especially with Matthew, the Old Testament itself. The matter becomes even stickier because some interpreters, like John and to some extent Paul, write interpretations without telling their readers what it is they are interpreting. I once drew a diagram showing with arrows who interpreted what and, with dotted lines, what can be compared with something else. By the time I finished, my paper was a mass of crisscrossed lines, and I felt more confused than the first time I played Tic-Tac-Toe in 3-D. I understood each move, considered by itself, but the whole configuration escaped me. Maybe you can do a better job with a diagram than I did. Trying to grasp as a whole the complex interrelations involved in a multiple text such as the love commandment raises the question: What does it all mean?

As our tour of the world of the love commandment draws to a close and we return again to everyday reality, we cease to look at the landscape from an aisle seat part-way back or from a window seat in front, and resume our usual outlook. Now here is a knotty question. What does it all mean—to whom, in which everyday reality, and by what usual outlook? The variety in any group and the multiplicity in each individual is a major variable in the interpretive process. We have to take ourselves into account in order to say what it all means.

In chapter 1, I said that interpretation has occurred when three things have happened:

1. A reader with an active mind and a full life has come to a story.
2. An imaginary tour of the world of the story has taken place.
3. The reader has appropriated the story, making it part of an enriched life.

We can check number one and number two off our list. We are now at number three. No amount of scholarship can make the love commandment part of your life or mine. The scholar's bag of tricks contains no magic answers, no coded maps. At this point I join my readers in the attempt to make the love commandment part of a life lived in several roles, through good days and bad ones, amidst a gaggle of commitments and values not altogether compatible. How should we go about the task of incorporating the love commandment into our lives? I have five more or less practical suggestions to assist in the process.

1. *Decide the level of generalization at which you want to incorporate the love commandment into your life.* Are you looking for political philosophy and professional ethics, or are you looking for a slogan to put on a plaque over the sink and on a bumpersticker for the car? I think a great deal of dissatisfaction with proposals for applying the love commandment can be avoided by clarifying this point.

Most discussions of the application of the love commandment that I have heard in churches limit the level of generalization to various kinds of face-to-face relations, such as family relations, youth fellowship meetings, church committees and boards, workplace relations with immediate coworkers, and the like. Such relations come under the formulation: "Love one another." This is an artificial limitation. The love commandment is presented in the New Testament as the criterion not only for those face-to-face relations from which one may expect mutual respect and support, but also for larger-scale relations where the norm is civility and cordiality, such as commercial dealings with the corner grocer and bureaucratic encounters with the Internal Revenue Service. The New Testament uses the term "neighbor" to cover these people with whom you are less personally involved. Most professional ethics and social action strategy belongs here.

In general, if the level of generalization takes you beyond the home and the congregation, the love commandment in the form "love one another" will not fit. You will need to think in terms of a neighbor with whom little mutual support is likely. This means you need to think of "Love your neighbor as yourself" in the way Leviticus 19:34 expressed it: treating outsiders as you like to be treated when you are outsiders or, alternatively, treating outsiders as you wish you had been treated when you were outsiders. I can't resist an example of professional ethics which contains a pun on "outsiders": After one and one-half hours in the waiting room, you begin to wish dentists treated those outside as well as they treat those in the chair!

2. *Decide what the relevant situation is and what your role is in the situation.* You will have better success, I think, if you take things one situation at a time. To define a situation, you might ask the question: Which of my roles is the one I play in this situation? Am I leader, parent, helper, consumer, spouse, thinker, educator, Christian, city-dweller, volunteer, or budget-balancer? Sorting out the roles should give contour and limits to the situation.

When you have identified the situation, its analysis should be easier. A key question in the analysis of the situation is: Is mutuality and reciprocity part of a realistic assessment of the situation? Or is this a situation of hostility? Or is it an impersonal situation with neither hostility nor reciprocity? Things are not always what they seem, you know. How long do you have to be around churches before you find that "love one another" is as much a goal as a reality? And isn't it the case that families fairly often fail to be places of mutuality? If mutuality is lacking, even temporarily, in the situation, you will be hurt and disillusioned if you expect understanding and support, or even recognition of your presence.

Here's an example. A friend of mine realized, after a period of hurt confusion, that the new pastor, who spoke frequently and warmly about love, was consistently ignoring her observations, denigrating her suggestions, rejecting her leadership, and generally tearing down her carefully-nurtured self-confidence. She tried being understanding, and she tried modifying her behavior to avoid threatening him. Eventually, she concluded that despite all the love-talk, the reality was that she was a victim. There was no mutuality in the situation, and living by the rule "love one another" simply continued a bad scene. It was necessary to improvise a way to restore communication and rebuild appropriate respect. She made an appointment with him at which she said something like this: "Pastor, I must do something that is very hard for me to do. I have to forgive you for tearing me down." Meanwhile she continued her participation in the life of the church.

I doubt that my friend and her pastor will ever be buddies, but I can report a restored relationship of mutual respect. What she did, it seems to me, was to analyze the situation as one of hostility and to follow Paul's formula in Romans 12:19-21. She really did turn the situation over to God and she continued to live the way church members ordinarily do, participating as usual in the life of the church. The burden of hostility was placed on the pastor; it became a matter between him and God, and he terminated his hostile behavior right away. This lengthy example is intended to underline the importance of correctly identifying the situation and your role in it.

3. *Be prepared to exercise your imagination.* In chapter 1 I enumerated some characteristic acts of imagination which we use, often without thinking

about it, whenever we hear a story. If you think of your life as one story and the love commandment as another story, you know that you can set the stories side by side, so that comparison will illuminate the course of the story you live. I call this interpretive strategy "juxtaposition" in chapter 1, although when I wrote it I was thinking about juxtaposing two Bible stories such as Matthew's and Luke's rather than the reader's and Luke's. Because your life is not one story but several, all mixed up together, and because the love commandment is not one story but several, somewhat disentangled by the excursion undertaken in this book, you know you will have to experiment to find the points at which the love commandment sheds the most light. Mixing and matching the segments and scenes of stories will require imagination.

Another act of the imagination, one you have already used, is the interpretive strategy I called "accumulation." While you read this book and took a tour of the world of the love commandment, you were adding the various interpretations of the love commandment to the top of your pile of "things to think about," bringing them one at a time and in varying combinations into conscious focus as a major criterion of your Christian life. There is no way to make any text in the whole Bible part of your life without testing in your imagination where it fits, what it challenges, what new possibilities it opens.

4. *Don't neglect the church.* It is the place where the Bible is studied and incorporated into Christian life and thought, the only place you'll ever meet people struggling with its meaning for today, the only place you'll find people who intend to focus all of their inner resources on God alone and who value a similar religious intensity in others. There are, of course, nooks and crannies of the church where the Bible is never studied or is studied by closed minds with unwarranted confidence that some recipe for Christian life and thought needs no modification. I'm no friend of those corners of the church. When I think of the church I apply the Noah's Ark rule: If you don't like the smell inside, think of the storm outside. The point is that outside the church, loving God isn't a high value and the Bible isn't studied and incorporated into Christian lives at all.

Wherever some passage of the Bible, such as the love commandment, is encountered and incorporated into Christian lives, the church is changed. When that passage is a multiple text, an interpretation of an interpretation of an interpretation, two specific changes can be traced. A multiple text such as the love commandment forces choices on readers, generates a variety of deeply-held convictions among readers, and creates a pluralistic church which advocates, in love, various things about what it means to love. Such lack of consensus is not immoral. It is, rather, a sign of the struggle to be faithful Christians in today's world, a struggle mandated by the multiplicity of the text itself. A multiple text, such as the love commandment, also creates a church which is democratic. The possibilities we glimpsed on our tour of the world of the love commandment, multiplied by the enormous variety of the roles we play and the questions and situations we bring to a text on any given day, reduces distinctions between experts and nonexperts, clergy and laity, maturity and youth. When it comes to incorporating the love commandment into Christian lives, we're all in it together.

5. *Return to the text.* How can we find its meaning for today? The final answer is that there is no substitute for returning to the source. Returning to the source need not mean returning to the same passages. In many other places in the Gospels, you can read instructions and commandments, parables and dialogues which give some idea of what Jesus meant by "love," what kind of content he gave to it. In the long run, it is likely that the earliest Christians thought the love commandment was important not only because Jesus said it, but also because he lived it. The crucifixion and resurrection speak volumes about the boundaries of love and about its self-sacrificial character, don't they?

Whenever we ran out of time before we finished exploring a familiar Bible passage, one member or another of a church school class I used to teach would say, "Well, we'll come back to it," which meant not only (1) "There will be Sunday school next week," but, more significantly, (2) "This isn't the first time in a lifetime of church-going we've thought about this passage and it won't be the last." My suspicion is that it also meant (3) "I've never heard anything so screwy in all my life." There is no single right interpretation of the love commandment for all people at all times and in all situations. There is only a faithful return to the source and fresh interpretation for today. I will count this book a success if a reader has pondered not the book itself, but the passages and interpretations and interconnections which make up the world of the love commandment. That kind of reading goes way beyond textbook exercises. I think it is fair to say that any such readers have loved the Lord with all their mind.

Appendix

Literary Approaches to the Study of the Bible

Biblical scholars have fought hard battles to gain their independence of ecclesiastical authorities and confessional prescriptions. Such scholars have often been earnest Christians with a deep love of the church. The battle is joined when the scholarly quest for the truth about the Bible runs into closed minds that know all they want to know or into documents which enshrine the wisdom of one century as if it were truth for all times. The lesson for us is clear: Scholarship must be free to pursue the truth wherever it leads. We who follow in their scholarly footsteps are much indebted to those pioneers who have broken the trail and are obligated by their example to stand in solidarity with biblical scholars engaged in similar battles in the present.

Meanwhile, biblical scholars who are not under siege ought not to have a siege mentality. To be sure, much work still must be done behind the closed doors of some ivory tower because only there can questions be asked which have no immediate, and perhaps no eventual, payoff for Christian faith. But secrecy is not a virtue. Where there is no siege, there is no reason to circle the wagons. We can afford to say what we know and, by and large, most of us are not afraid to. For some decades now both the methods and the results of historical criticism have been taught openly in colleges and seminaries. Generations of seminary students have filled notebooks full of what biblical scholars know. Some of those students have figured out how to pass along these treasures to congregations. Others have not.

Figuring out how to pass along what biblical scholars know is too important a task to be dumped in the laps of former seminary students armed only with notebooks left over from their seminary days. It results in too much work at cross-purposes, too much wasted effort on all sides. Biblical scholarship itself must take up the task. The question biblical scholars need to address is: What items of what we know should we say to whom and in what order? Scholars are often fascinated by social and political events at which texts hint, the religious milieu of the original audience, wonderful old texts found somewhere or other which may contain fascinating secrets or useful trivia, and the like. What interests us may not interest the church. Or it may interest the church in a different way and for some different reason. It is possible that the basic research which is high on our agenda ought not to be on the church's agenda at all. The agenda of the church, and the place where ecclesiastical and scholarly agendas coincide, is the study of texts in the Bible. Is there some systematic way to do our work that will result in transmitting what we know and are learning, ready for use?

What I have written in this little book is something of a trial run, testing the capacity to communicate of approaches which are being called "literary." I hope that out of the discussion now in progress among biblical scholars about "literary interpretation of biblical literature," there will emerge a scholarly method which will unite academy, pulpit, and pew in a fruitful engagement with the Bible.

I have not given up on historical criticism. I am quite conscious that I have used text criticism, source criticism, form criticism, redaction criticism, and perhaps other methods in common use among biblical scholars. It seems clear to me that an ancient document has to be investigated historically. How else? Literary methods which fail to take into account the original settings of the text are not suitable for biblical interpretation, in my view.

The chief value of literary method is its capacity to focus attention on the story or argument of a text. What I like is being able to begin with a story and end with the same story much enriched. I'm not greatly impressed with how different antiquity is from our own day. Even if I were, I would not be locked out. All literature sets out a world and invites the reader to enter. A little data, carefully selected, goes a long way in opening a passage for reading in today's world. If you want to find the meaning of a text for today, you need a method which focuses on texts, not on something else.

The second major value I see in literary method is its capacity to eliminate a second step in interpretation. I am thinking of this scheme: Step One: historical critical analysis; Step Two: application for today. With literary method, there is only one step: reading the text. Such reading trusts literature to speak and insists, by disciplined listening, on letting it speak in its own voice. I do not propose to examine here the role of the preacher in single-step interpretation using literary methods. Suffice it to say that the people in the pews bear relatively more responsibility for the interpretation than is usually the case and the preacher relatively less. The preacher, as speaker, represents the readers as together they tour the world of the text, incorporating it into their lives as they go along.

Here is a list of the ways I find literary criticism helpful in interpretation.

1. *Literary criticism values the variety of meanings which are legitimately to be found in any text.* It makes it possible for two Christians to disagree on the interpretation of the Bible without one of them having to be wrong. There are, of course, wrong answers, things a particular passage can't possibly mean, no matter how earnest the interpreter. No text has only one meaning, on the one hand; only a finite range of meanings is possible, on the other.

2. *Literary criticism values the multiplicity in any text.* This is especially important in the New Testament where the same saying often appears several times. There is no particular literary reason to value most highly the oldest form of a tradition. Nor is there reason to begin, as I did, with the earliest Gospel.

3. *Literary criticism allows meanings to spill over from one text to another.* I traced this process in chapter 2 to show the mutual influence of Deuteronomy 6:4-5 and Leviticus 19:18. In the same way Deuteronomy 6:4-5 appears legitimately in the interpretation of Paul, whether he had ever heard the two verses quoted together. The legitimacy and limits of the spilling over of meaning from one passage to another requires further theoretical consideration than is possible here.

4. *Literary criticism permits and even encourages comparisons on a grand scale.* For literary criticism it is not necessary that two things be related historically or conceptually before they can be compared. The act of interpretation itself is, in some ways, a matter of comparing your life to some text or other and keeping at it until it clicks. It is at this point that biblical scholars become frightened of bizarre comparisons which the history of interpretation shows are all too likely to be put forth. There are limits to comparisons, to be sure, and we lack definitions, both in theory and in practice, of those limits. Caution is certainly in order in this hazardous matter.

5. *Literary criticism permits changing your mind and, in this way, encourages taking chances on interpretations that may have to be changed.* Given the case of the multiple reader and the case of the multiple text discussed in this book, how could a single interpretation be the final word, never to be changed?

What I have, in fact, written in this book uses literary criticism rather cautiously and relies very heavily on reasonably standard historical-critical methods. In general, I have used literary methods for heuristic purposes and historical-critical methods for basic analysis of passages. There are, however, points at which my analysis differs from that of historical critics: I compared Paul with the Gospels; I didn't even mention the problem of a Q version of the love commandment; I assumed without much ado that "love one another" and various other phrases refer to Leviticus 19:18; I interpreted the parable of the good Samaritan and the dialogue in which it is embedded as a unit; I often found Deuteronomy 6:4-5 to be present where only Leviticus 19:18 was quoted.

Notes

Chapter 1
The three-phase theory of interpretation owes considerable debt to the thought of Paul Ricoeur. The appendix at the end of the book discusses the relation between historical and literary method further. William A. Beardslee, *Literary Criticism of the New Testament,* Guides to Biblical Scholarship (Philadelphia: Fortress, 1969) is a basic work.

I have used the Revised Standard Version, second edition, 1971, throughout.

Chapter 2
The criteria for distinguishing sayings of the historical Jesus may be found in Norman Perrin, *Rediscovering the Teachings of Jesus* (New York: Harper and Row, 1976). Robert L. Banks, *Jesus and the Law in the Synoptic Tradition,* Society for New Testament Studies Monograph Series 28 (Cambridge: University Press, 1975) treats the historical Jesus. David Daube, *The New Testament and Rabbinic Judaism* (London: Athlone Press, 1956) contains provocative material relevant to this chapter and those which follow.

The two Old Testament passages, Deuteronomy 6:4-5 and Leviticus 19:18, are treated in commentaries, of which some standard works are Gerhard von Rad, *Deuteronomy,* The Old Testament Library (Philadelphia: Westminster, 1966) and Martin Noth, *Leviticus,* The Old Testament Library (Philadelphia: Westminster, 1965) They are also treated in Dale Patrick, *Introduction to Biblical Law* (Atlanta: John Knox, 1984).

Three books on the love commandment in the New Testament have been published recently. All three are usable and helpful; the first is the easiest to read. These include Pheme Perkins, *Love Commands in the New Testament* (Ramsey, N.J.: Paulist Press, 1982); Luise Schottroff, Reginald H. Fuller,

Christoph Burchard, and M. Jack Suggs, *Essays on the Love Commandment* (Philadelphia: Fortress, 1978); John Piper, *Love Your Enemies,* Society for New Testament Studies Monograph Series 38 (Cambridge: University Press, 1979).

Anders Nygren's *Agape and Eros* (Reprint edition, Chicago: University of Chicago, 1982) is a standard historical and theological work on the subject of this book.

Chapter 3

The basic commentary on Mark is still Vincent Taylor, *The Gospel According to Mark* (London: Macmillan and Co., 1959). Introductions treat the issues of the composition of the Gospels and the priority of Mark. Norman Perrin, *The New Testament: An Introduction,* 2nd edition with Dennis C. Duling (New York: Harcourt Brace Jovanovich, 1982), and Helmut Koester, *Introduction to the New Testament,* Vol. 2 (Philadelphia: Fortress, 1982) are new and excellent. W.G. Kümmel, *Introduction to the New Testament* (Nashville: Abingdon, 1975) is the standard work.

Chapter 4

Matthew's view of law is subtle and has attracted considerable scholarly attention. Several contributions to *Essays on the Love Commandment,* a book referred to in the notes for chapter 2, concern Matthew's discussion. Other standard works are W.D. Davies, *The Setting of the Sermon on the Mount* (Cambridge: University Press, 1977), and Gerhard Barth, "Matthew's Understanding of the Law" in *Tradition and Interpretation in Matthew,* edited by Günther Bornkamm, Gerhard Barth, and Heinz-Joachim Held (Philadelphia: Westminster, 1963).

Chapter 5

My interpretation of the parable of the good Samaritan owes a considerable debt to the work of R.W. Funk, especially in *Language, Hermeneutic and Word of God* (New York: Harper and Row, 1966). *Semeia 2,* edited by John Dominic Crossan (Missoula: Scholars Press, 1974), contains several articles on the good Samaritan, including one by Funk.

The classics of research on parables are C.H. Dodd, *The Parables of the Kingdom,* originally published in 1935 and available in several editions, and Joachim Jeremias, *The Parables of Jesus,* first translated into English in 1954 and also available in several editions. More recently, within the Society of Biblical Literature, a seminar on the parables has produced vigorous discussion reflected in a number of publications. Among these are several volumes of the Semeia series and several significant books, among which I mention only Mary Ann Tolbert, *Perspectives on the Parables: An Approach to Multiple Interpretations* (Philadelphia: Fortress, 1979).

Chapter 6

The most recent commentary is by Raymond E. Brown, *The Gospel of John,* Anchor Bible, Vols. 29 and 29A (New York: Doubleday, 1966, 1970). The most recent monograph is by R. Alan Culpepper, *Anatomy of the*

Fourth Gospel: A Study in Literary Design, Foundations and Facets (Philadelphia: Fortress, 1983).

Chapter 7

Every few years a major monograph about Paul is published. Reviews in magazines will assist the reader in locating them. The most recent are Wayne Meeks, *The First Urban Christians* (New Haven: Yale, 1983) and J. Christiaan Beker, *Paul the Apostle* (Philadelphia: Fortress, 1980).

Concerning 1 Corinthians: Hans Conzelmann's commentary in the Hermeneia series (Philadelphia: Fortress, 1975) and Gerd Theissen, *The Social Setting of Pauline Christianity* (Philadelphia: Fortress, 1982).

Concerning Galatians: Hans-Dieter Betz' commentary in the Hermeneia series (Philadelphia: Fortress, 1979).

Concerning Romans: Ernst Käsemann, *Commentary on Romans* (Grand Rapids: Wm. B. Eerdmans, 1980).